Libel and Slander Of Angela C. Williams

By Angela C. Williams

ISBN 10 - 1514360454
ISBN 13 - 9781514360453

Dedication

To Jesus, Booker T. Staten Sr., Sophonia Staten, Herman King Williams Sr., Minerva Williams, Christine Staten Williams, Jerry C. Williams, Carlos J. Williams, Indigo Skye Harper, Kyle Williams, **Malakhi Harper**, Lorine Pickett, Sophonia Staten II, Matthew Lorenzo Pickett Jr., my English/Literature teachers; all of my family/friends, everyone who gave me a dollar when I was homeless, (speaking by faith), and Police officers.

CONTENTS

ACKNOWLEDGMENTS

Thank You to all of those strangers who give me a dollar when I humbly ask; since I've been homeless. Thank you to my daughter. Thank you to those who have helped me without me knowing. Thank you to you for purchasing this book.

Chapter 1

Introduction

Now if you aren't familiar with the counties in New York, like myself; you may not understand the significance of mentioning my mother's maiden name; Staten and my father's hometown; Richmond. Maybe they're pronouncing it incorrectly but we spell it the same. Staten Island is a city inside the state of New York. Richmond is a county inside the state of New York that happens to be where Staten Island is located.

You have to wonder if our families were the first to be brought over on the slave ships. Or maybe African-Americans got here before Christopher Columbus (Lol). Yes I read all of my History text books and I passed with flying colors but I can't seem to remember, a section about the history of New York City. If we think about it, I suppose the entire eastern shore of our country probably holds a vast amount of information regarding blood-lines, marriages and slave papers. Well I would log onto Ancestry.com, however, I do not have a credit card and I have no money in my bank account. I do not have the ability to leave this place where I'm sleeping because I do not have a key. I'm stuck in here until my daughter gets here; at which time I must leave and go pan-handle so that I'm able to pay my health insurance (monthly) premium, storage fees, cost of groceries or toiletries and anything else you would need cash to do; yes I'm unemployed and homeless. She doesn't want her son on the bus and I do not have a car. I agree, it's not safe for him on the bus. But it's also not conducive to my well-being to be stuck here, not able to handle issues with my health insurance payment coming straight out of my account and other issues of the sort. (Every dollar I received this week went into my account to pay for basic health coverage). I'm practically being held against my will. I'm watching my first and only grandson for free; that is actually a joy. Not to be misunderstood; I don't blame my daughter. She's probably being paid by my rich, former friends to hold me here.

Understand. Even if I tell her to get another babysitter and move back in to the hotel, I'll be in a situation where I'm held against my will. I will be pan-handling full-time. Working a regular job is not an option because of conditioning and harassment. When I'm here with her, she refuses to hold a conversation with me; at all (every day). She thinks I'm the enemy because our ungodly former friends and family separated us and left us without shelter. She may have also begun believing the "I'm a ho" non-sense like the rest of the human population. I love my daughter dearly and I will always help her if I'm able.

More so than becoming a doctor, attorney or teacher; I pray that I'm able to teach my grandson how to be a God-fearing, kind man who loves his wife, children and his friends and family. Most of all, a man who loves himself so much that he treats others the way he treats himself. I'm trying to give my daughter a chance to have a prosperous life. I'm appreciative of the time I have to get some writing done because it has always been a longing desire of mine to do so. But I had other goals and plans in mind for myself after my daughter graduated from high school. I was headed to Florida to write books or articles on the beach during the day and waiting tables in the evening. I desire to join a bowling league and raise money for walk-a-thons. I wanted to bond with my brother; now that we are older. She needs my help and my grandson needs my love and protection. Going to college while maintaining a child and a job is not an easy task.

There is not one time during the 6 years that I've been homeless that I have been in a 'back slidden' state. I figured church would have had many helpful programs. I tried to go to several different churches, but something wasn't right. These so called programs were never offered and unlike the unsaved people on the street, no one offered me a place to rest. I'd established residence in a hotel with a kitchen and it took, all morning to get the (other half of the) money before 11am, that day, to pay for the room. I didn't want my daughter in a shelter. I was sometimes able to call a church and leave a message explaining my situation. Sometimes they would send someone to pay for a week or so. I sent out mass mailings to churches.

It was as if some kind of strange, gossip induced stupor had fallen upon the minds of everyone in every House of God. I married at 22 to honor God. I did not grow less aware of the importance and purpose of marriage as I aged. We didn't have a large savings account but we had large hearts and a lot of determination; exactly what most Black marriages of the past were built upon. God is God and love is love, no matter what century we find ourselves.

To be one of the races who give more change and dollars to homeless folks in need, blacks sure are a cold, mean, cynical race of people who sure do have a knack for crushing a person's aspirations. Everyone needs love and friendship; and everyone desires to prosper.

I'm not a liar and I'm not a ho. If you're a movie/TV buff, this book is for you.

What if an aspiring artist chose to write a TV show called The House of Payne using a specific person's name to tell a story of a black woman who used to be a crack addict. What if the entire world just arbitrarily believes it's someone else with a completely different name- because a few other facts in the show make you think about her instead. (One of the reasons why my daughter stopped cheering is because the little boys on the field must have been told by their parents that I was a drug addict). They walked up to me and called me a crack addict. The other mothers were trying to use their children to harass me away from the field. A fat girl from my old neighborhood who happens to have the same name as the crack addict in the TV show, walked up to me one day and said, you used to do drugs; and then she walked away. What do you think it could be that causes someone to just replace the name and events in his or her mind and act upon their beliefs as if the information in a TV show is regarding a completely different person? Am I delusional or are they delusional?

Oh, I get it. That's why the male actor from The House of Payne, who was married to the crack addict, had my (HS freshman year) jersey number on in his old TV show, A different World or The Cosby show; because he really represents me and this is your way of saying, ("I'm the man"), and a specific guy I'm dating, has done; or is doing, drugs. That is straight up sabotage. Misery loves company.

Now let the hospital emergency room tell it, and I'd done drugs. Since I'd been homeless, that is. If it was in my system it must have gotten there because I had sex and/or kissed a man who had done drugs or taken a puff of some sort. I did not know that my male friend in which I'd been in an on/off relationship with for approximately 7 years or so, used to do drugs; until I overheard a guy mention it while I was sitting in the barbershop one day talking to a friend of mine. He apparently stopped, when our relationship began. But what's ironic about this, is that everyone, including the men and women whom I know that work in the healthcare field, the theology field and the 'humanitarian field'; left me outside. You want a good laugh? She treats a homeless person in the emergency room when they don't feel well; then spreads a nasty rumor that they smell like they wore their clothes two days in a row. Can you believe they actually found other people willing to make it seem like that's a worthy argument to tell the massive heathen population. You are in the business of caring and saving lives. Buy him or her an outfit, some food and give them bus fare. If I was in an emergency room and I smelled sweaty or like my clothes had been worn twice, it had to be a first; an extenuating circumstance.

Now in the news this week, is a story about a woman who, when she was alive, had one of the strongest singing voices around. She was beautiful. I happened to catch a movie today about her singing career. She was wearing a very familiar patterned scarf on her head. It was identical to the leotard that I wore during dance practice when I was 14 years old. This woman supposedly drowned in the bathtub due to a drug overdose, not too long ago. During the last years of her life, she had been in and out the news for drug addiction.

I have never smoked a cigarette or marijuana. I've never abused (or used) drugs or alcohol. I have never taken nor do I believe I need to take, medication for my mind.

Even though I believe I'm of sound mind and body; it's hard to make your mark on the world when you're constantly reacting to obstacles that you didn't know were sabotage until it was too late to tell the truth.

For every one person whom you believe I slept with without truly dating first, there are 4 to 5 others whom I said no to that wanted to pressure me into a physical situation. And for every two women who didn't invite me out, hug me or talk to me regularly, there were at least two males who did invite me out; so we dated; and they never tried to touch me at all. For every man who I've dated there are 5 women who I'd rather be hanging out with. Job, school or church; this is the gospel truth. Put your thinking cap on. The issue is that if a man heard that a few other men, had treated a woman a certain way, then in their mind, they should treat the woman the same way. Now how would they know, unless you tell them? Oh, I guess the TV told them. All of the stories told, are negative. Who's telling the positive stories so that the man can say wow, men sure treat her kindly; I will too. No one is telling those stories because those people don't gossip (and start rumors). Which one do you choose to be? I don't try penis' out to see if someone is 'good'. For the people who read this paragraph and still think I'm a ho; I have to wonder if you aren't mentally challenged. (Or maybe love challenged). In my heart and mind, even if I'm intimate with a man who is still married on paper, I expect dating and marriage. (I know that's wrong in God's eyes but now I have brain damage from

lack of communicating with people. You forced me to befriend such people. Liars and pretenders.) And yes I prefer to date first before intimacy. In all honesty, that hasn't always been the case).That doesn't mean I didn't get to know them. I'd also prefer to be married before intimacy. Even more; I'd prefer to just have friends and no intimacy. I guess I could always just sit and stare at the wall until I die. I'd rather try to develop lasting relationships with other humans. Think about what I'm saying. But it may be hard for you to think the way I think, if you are not saved, if you are whore-minded, if you are uneducated, or if you are not very nice. I've known my former girlfriends for over 30 years and I never thought they would revoke their friendship.

Just in case you aren't aware; my married last name was Harper. No I'm not a man and no I didn't sleep with anyone on my (former Pro-football player) ex-husband's side of the wedding party. But many folks seem to think I look a lot like my father, especially around the nose; and the bride in this particular movie. Never have been the matron of Honor, but I guess I could be *The Best Man.* Nothing in either of The Best Man movies, is a reflection of something I've said or done. But a female Federal Police Officer and former basketball team-mate of mine, told me that my best friend from high school was married and her husband left her. I was in her wedding. The dresses are identical to those in the movie, *The Best Man.* I don't know if she is being set-up or not. But I know, I am. 'She's the bride', but she's wearing my face. The infamous author in the movie goes by my married surname. And his friends are a little upset that he's told their stories, along with his own, but changed their names. (No one lives in the world alone). Are they telling me I'm about to die in the movie, *The Best Man Holiday*? I now must spend the rest of my life trying to justify my existence; and I'm the one being lied on. I'm not lying on anyone.

You know, I seriously don't understand any humans argument (in a debate on the matter) that someone would not want to have a permanent roof over their head with familiar company; be in a committed relationship with a like-minded person; would not want to go out and enjoy life and all its culture with their friends; and would not want to stay healthy and disease-free.

I know this story would be much more exciting if I was telling you that for the past 20 years I've been married to my high school sweetheart who is truly in love with me. We work out 3x a week and right now we are butt naked on a chair and his big penis is deep inside my vagina while he sucks on my double D titty's right before we jumped into the shower to get ready for our $60,000 dollar per year, jobs. (And when we got in the shower, he grabbed my waist and did it to me from the back)........... ok, ok I'm getting a little carried away; but you get my point. Well, be happy, that's your life and who wants to read about themselves. Live a little.

Many years ago when I was in college, I shared with my green-eyed friend that I wanted to start a book club. He was the only one I told; (over the phone). He now owns a Fitness Club in Florida. You know the chubby, black woman with her own talk show and magazine; it's ironic that this friend I speak of, looks very similar to; and shares the same name as; this media mogul's hair stylist. Go figure.

I'm not very well-read so they wouldn't give me my own talk show but it sure would be fun. My prosperous career may have never come to fruition but I do know quite a bit; love to do research and could facilitate a debate show with my hands tied behind my back.

I don't read a lot of books leisurely now because I am a writer and I did not want to be influenced or directed to write a certain way.

Either everybody is really, really dumb or extremely mean. As individuals, we have control over what we choose to focus on. You can spend your entire life looking for all of the things that you consider mistakes in a person's life or you can spend your entire life documenting all of their noble acts and note-worthy accomplishments. In this sense, media can make a person, or destroy their character.

I'm being blamed for other people's sins. I am not a ho now; nor did I used to be. I don't sell sex now, nor did I used to, nor will I later. The unfortunate part is that you probably won't believe any of what I say. If I were you, I wouldn't believe me either. And the reason why I wouldn't believe me, is because if I were you; I would have already been brain washed for (20 odd years), into believing that I'm the unlikable character in every movie/TV program. They put someone else in my clothing, and show a few correct details about me, then tell some outlandish story that is either true about someone else (or others), or it's completely made up; they show one specific detail in two unrelated movies to make you believe that what they're saying must be true.   It's too bad that my mother was so giving. Our family gave thousands of dollars worth of our clothing to American Rescue Workers. Now proving that I wore those outfits would have to be accomplished through photos or credit card receipts.

That's TV. But it was the radio that created the image of me being a cheater in everyone's mind.

Everyone believes everything they've seen is true and that it's about me. My kindness has been mocked and sabotaged. My loyalty has been twisted and manipulated into something unthinkable in a world that doesn't even really exist.

When someone has believed a lie for so long; when they hear the truth, it's much easier to continue pretending that the lie is really the truth because it's easier than saying they were wrong. Instead of saying, gosh, for 10 years I've believed that scene in those two movies was about you; they'll say, "Well who was it then"? Do you see the ignorance in that?

It's cold, dark and rainy. I had no money and no place to sleep. I was sitting alone, outside at the laundromat, in the chair with no laundry to be washed. There was no one else there. Just the attendant who was working that evening. Oh yeah and a dirty homeless looking white guy with long hair. I figured he was probably a movie producer spying on me. If you were me, what would you be thinking? If I were you, what would I be thinking? I definitely wouldn't be thinking that you were a ho sitting there without a pimp or a client. Yes, there were several nights when I just slept sitting in that chair.

(It's like everyone would rather see me catch a case and watch my future fade away). Yes. Standing in front of a judge for pan-handling, is a court-case. It also makes me shake my head when I hear songs that seem to express the sentiment I feel but the artist is getting richer from my demise. No I don't know them so I do not expect them to send me money; but still. Why don't the husbands of the women singing sexy lyrics, think they're ho's? Oh, because they believe all of them are singing about me.

I'm not 5 years old. Yes men act ignorant sometimes when it comes to love and commitment. But this book is not about my feelings being hurt; not even by a man. This is about years of intentional libel and slander that has led to a slow death for me and some others in my family. Attempted Murder!

If the Black women who stay involved with the local Boys and Girls Club as a youth, acquire a Bachelor's degree from a 4 year college without taking out a loan, join a Christian sorority, pay their way through hair school, marry at 22 (and then have a child), change career fields to education so they can give back to our youth, travel without waiting for a man to invite them and volunteer in their community; are the ones we consider ho's, we might want to check ourselves. My Real-life is the way it is because of the mess on television and on the radio; no doubt.

Adventures in Homelessness

My late grandfather from Emporia, was a pastor. (Yes I began to believe at an early age that Jesus Christ died for my sins. I believe that he rose again and ascended into heaven to sit at the right hand of Father God. I believe that I am filled with His precious Holy Spirit. The Father, The Son and The Holy Spirit; The Trinity. I was saved, (protected from eternal damnation), when I confessed this from my mouth at an early age. He and my grandmother got married and began their family at ages 14 and 15. They had 8 children. Five boys and three girls. Once the oldest, my uncle Booger; (Booker T); moved up here, everybody else followed. We all attended Refreshing Springs COGIC; both sides of my family. Well, my mother passed away about 12 years ago. Forty (40) years is a long time to be married to someone. I'm sure it is difficult for my father to be without my mom. I just kind of thought my father would put more energy into my daughter after I lost my job. He's helping her now but it's pretty much too late. He should have helped me when she because she was still in grade school then. I thought we would be living with him. Well, long story short, he has a new female friend and she has a daughter with the same name as me. She is a doctor. His lady friend was the nanny for her daughter's children. My father had begun going to church on a regular basis ever since my mother had been sick. But he soon moved south, by himself.

My daughter and I had our own apartment for a little while but I was not being called for substitute assignments quite as often and I was being verbally harassed. I broke my lease and was blessed enough to be able to move in with my aunt, our cousins and their children. My daughter and I were creating more of a crowd than there already was but we were comfortable. It may have worked out if my older, much bigger, male cousin hadn't lost his temper and struck me upside my head for apparently saying something that hurt his mother's feelings.

Now mind you, I've managed at this point, to get through 17 years of school without being in a fight. (Before it was all said and done, I had been physically assaulted by two family members in two separate homes in which she and I stayed and by two women in two different houses where we rented a room.) No there was no fight. I just pressed charges. No blood or bruises; but still. No, I'm not sassing people because I'm upset; I swear. There must have been something in the water in that region.

The person who randomly hit my younger cousin over the head with a pole and left him for dead on the sidewalk at the Blvd shopping Center, must have had some of the same water. My cousin later died of blunt force trauma to his brain. He was a student at the community college and he was employed. He used to live in the home of the family that took us in when we became homeless. My aunt's grandson. Here was an example of an extended family who all stayed in the same home to give everyone a chance at a better life, while enjoying each other's company. The exact opposite of our extended family situation, where we all lived in different states. I guess both situations could be beneficial and rewarding but it all nullified when we are all being sabotaged in one way or another. Some say that's just life. I beg to differ.

My father traveled back up to our area quite frequently. He and his friend invited me and my daughter to attend a Nutcracker performance at Maryland University one holiday season after we all attended church. After all of this; I still found myself with no place to sleep. I just couldn't fathom why. It was too late to get the money for a room. I spent that night outside. The next day, I pan-handled and got a hotel room. (Everyone else believes I'm crazy)? I think there's something wrong with everyone else. If I knew she was going to allow him to leave me outside before he 'hit the road' to head back south, and she wasn't going to come pick me up, I would have stayed at the church. I needed money on a daily basis and it was difficult to spend the time traveling to and focusing on church. I prayed, praised and worshipped in my hotel room.

My daughter and I did not deserve to have to go through this non sense.

Before I became homeless, I was struggling to turn my credit around, keep my career flourishing and provide a fun safe environment for my daughter. As a single parent, when she was 4, I enrolled her in a private, Christian pre-school. I ended up not being able to afford it because I left my job. (Clearly my intentions were right). I changed careers and worked the stressful job of managing 35 -40 kids at once, for 7 years in a classroom setting. This job allowed me to spend much more time with her. I drove her to the North Beach, Ocean City, Watkin's Park Petting Zoo, rode bikes through trails, we rode bikes and played mini-golf at Hain's Point. When she was just 5 years old, we dressed up and drove downtown to the theatre to see a Scooby Doo play. I took her to the park and pitched softballs to her. I took her to bowl duck pins at the local alley while I bowled by myself. We explored the National Zoo down-town. I played frisbee with her in my father's backyard. I took my daughter to the park to play tennis, using the rackets my parents got for my brother and I when we were young. When she was ten, I even drove her to Miami to visit with my brother. My closest female cousin went with us. She shares the name of the woman who sang "I'd have all the money in the world, if I was a wealthy girl." I feel bad for her because she wanted like any other woman, to marry and have children. She's my age. She never married and she can no longer have children. Men are just scum).

Well, back to our road trip.....

Unfortunately I couldn't afford to take her to Disney World. (Wouldn't that break your heart if you were a kid?) We drove right past the park on our way to my brother's ex-wife's home. At least she got to swim in the in-door pool (at their home), with all of the other more fortunate children. (OK they may think she's more fortunate to have her birth mom with her; they're foster kids.) I'm so mad at his ex. She didn't even invite us to live with her. I had been approved for a home loan in North Carolina. Then I lost my job. My daughter was a great cheerleader with a community Boys and Girls Club. I remember going to Maryland University to watch my daughter in her cheerleading competition. I am very sad that I don't have more extracurricular activities to recall. I am very disappointed and angry with anyone who was in a position to keep this from happening to us.

My daughter was a middle-schooler who was in need of my guidance and direction. I had to leave my daughter there at my aunt's after my cousin struck me because I wasn't sure where I was going to go. She was well into the school year in that particular rural city. She didn't think I cared about her. Without my consent, the family members whom she was forced to stay with, let her go to a teen-age club with her little girlfriends. This is where she met her first boyfriend. Thank God she was covered by the Blood of Jesus. Even if I didn't pled it over her, I'm sure her father did.

Thank God I was covered by the blood of Jesus as well. I am claustrophobic! I cannot go to jail! I would be standing on the median with my homeless sign, then see a cop and run to the sidewalk. Once I did that and the cop made me sit down on the dirty curb, he called in a report, right in front of the Andrews main gate. I was standing there on purpose, hoping that someone would see me on the outdoor cameras and tell the president. I was thinking he might inquire as to why I was there and then help me. The cop checked my very small, vintage (1989) coach bag and it had $3,000 inside. (It was little and it could go across my body. And it could hook onto your belt if you wanted.) At this time my daughter still wasn't with me yet so I was able to stay with strangers sometimes, to save money (not once did I sell sex or sleep with them). I got a ticket but he didn't arrest me. It was terrifying. Even after the letters I'd written to the police chief and some politicians, some cops still approached me. There eventually came a time when the cops gave up. (Like now; years later). "Why did they finally give up,"? You're asking. One reason might be because I'm not going to become a hooker. The other reason might be because a cop stopped me from pan handling and coincidentally he was shot dead. Maybe it wasn't related, but; he mocked me, saying, "Why are you out her? I don't want to see you out here anymore." As if to imply that I was a ho and should stay inside. He was young and really nice. (Too bad he was misled). Even if he wasn't necessarily misled; what he said was very hurtful. (Another senseless death of a young black man).

With no savings I didn't have much choice. I called everyone whose number I had; (at least 20 people). No one would come and pick me up. No one came! I thought I was 'being punked'.

As I walked around outside, pan-handling, I was frequently asked how I became homeless. Well, let me tell you. I stood in my classroom upset that I had to keep repeating myself to the same misbehaving young boys. I sent PS-74 forms down to the vice principal. The boys would not stop. Thankfully, earlier that day, the department head had recommended that I send them to her room toward the end of the day as not to disturb the other peaceful children from dismissal. Before I had a chance to do that, these two boys began to strong arm each other and they nearly knocked me over. I turned around and smacked the boy on his arm. I was called down to the office the next day to give a statement. I saw the PS-74s still sitting in the vice-principals box. I was given a non-paid leave of absence until there was an investigation. Five to six months later, I received a letter stating that I was being let go. No, I didn't get an attorney. And no, I didn't call the boy's mother. I let it go.

I remembered that since taking the job, I had filed a small claims lawsuit against the board of education for verbal harassment. It was dismissed before it got to court, due to a technicality. But that may have had something to do with why I was let go as well; (after the investigation).

An investigative, federal police officer friend of mine who was concerned about my situation; offered for me to sleep in his grandmother's basement for the night until we could figure something else out. As we drove there, ironically, we passed my cousins house. I didn't say anything about that. They have allowed the roaches to take complete control of the house. He and I watched a movie and then we fell asleep. I was on one end of the bed, he was on the other. He eventually went upstairs to sleep somewhere else I guess. We were friends for a good little while. No we've never had sex. I was only able to stay there one night. We had been friends even before I'd given up my last apartment. I think he liked me. But I didn't feel that way. So, eventually he stopped calling. I think he actually changed his number. This situation is not about me being pressed for a man. It's not about me sleeping with people because I think they're cute or because I think it's what they want in order for me to stay there. That's not the point.

Even though I was able to stay in a hotel, some folks' random acts of kindness allowed me to save money. I'd decided to try sitting on the waist high wall at the local post-office as my method of discreetly asking for money. Of course I saw a lot of the same people pass-by every day. PO Boxes and such. I remember some of the men who offered me their phone numbers and told me to call if the night fell and I was still outside.

I slept on the sofa of a guy who seemed very scary. He drove a Metro Access bus and had a very frisky cat. I don't really like cats too much. I stayed for a few days but didn't really feel comfortable. He went out for New Year's and I just slept in and watched the ball drop. He came home drunk and scared me to death. The next day I sat outside again. No we did not sleep together.

Another guy whom I met at the same post-office. He was an older guy who shared with me that he was a substitute teacher in Montgomery County. He offered me rest in his spare room for a few days. He told me that he had daughters that were a little older than me, who lived out of town. The room was across the hall from the hallway bathroom. The bathroom had every item that a woman needed to have a luxurious bath and relax and smell real good. I was even able to wash a load of clothes. Unfortunately he went to run an errand the next day and I realized I was locked in the house. His doors lock from the inside and outside with a key. There's no turning switch on the inside. OK. That was the last night I stayed there. We spoke every time he came to the post-office. No I did not sleep with him; or anything of the sort.

17

For a while I stood at the drive-thru at a McDonalds in the city where I'd grown up. This was actually a good idea because this is where I'd gotten an apartment when I first came home. Maybe those who thought the men visiting were clients, would see the truth. One of the guys was the brother of the 2 sisters who are now doctors. He was helping me move my furniture. He passed away right before my mom.

There was a man who I'd met while standing with my sign at McDonald's. He offered his spare room for one night. He lived across the street from the mall where I began pan-handling; not far from the McDonald's.

I'm not sure where I met the gentleman who lived in Largo and offered me his sofa for a while. His car was filthy, on the inside. OMG. But he was very kind. He went to bed and I heard him weeping. I think he must have either expected me to sleep in his room or he was very sad about something else. I forgot to pray for him but I went to sleep and caught a ride back into town the next morning. Up bright and early to pan-handle all day. I stayed for a week or so I believe. No touching of any sort.

When I first ended up leaving my aunt's I wasn't sure where I would go. I was in the grocery store buying a few items for my hotel room and the man in front of me, was apologetic for taking so long in the self-check-out. He ended up paying for my groceries. That was really kind. He gave me his number and we talked briefly. I shared my situation and he came to my hotel to bless me with $20. We talked and I found out that he had a wife and 8 children. They lived in an apartment near the club where I temporarily worked. He sat on my bed in the hotel, where we talked some more. No we didn't kiss or anything. We are still cordial to this day when I see him or one of his triplet brothers, or his wife. He and his wife were kind enough to invite me to stay with them for a few months before I began sleeping on the sound guy's sofa. "What sound guy"? The guy from the club where I worked as a waitress for about 5 months after losing my teaching job.

There was a guy who had an apartment across the street from the mall where I began pan-handling. He offered me his sofa for 1 week. He had to go out of town for something but when he got back he offered me his sofa again. I stayed there another time on the night of the Super- Bowl. He asked me to go back and sit at the laundromat so he could invite another woman over to watch the game. When she left, he said, I could come back. The next time I stayed I was calling the only male I was really supposed to be talking to at the time. We were still talking although we'd had a disagreement about me wanting to go out more. I was no longer able to live at his sister's where he stayed sometimes too. He lived with his cousin. (You know; the rule. One friend at a time). But when he realized that I was calling another guy from his home phone, he said if I didn't have sex with him, then I had to leave. So I left. I see him around every now and again. We speak and then go on our way. No, we've never had sex.

I met a regular Metro bus driver who offered me his sofa. I was able to watch movies in his room until he came home. Then I hopped on the sofa. I think I just stayed one night. The next morning he went to a cook-out and my aunt came to pick me up and give me a ride to an area where I would be able to pan-handle. No we didn't sleep together. Nothing happened.

I'm not sure how I met the next guy but I remember him telling me that he was legally blind; however, he was driving. He had very thick glasses. I stayed with him for several days. He slept on the sofa and offered me his bed. He was very nice. He played retro music and we danced in the living room. I cooked and we watched TV. During the day, he worked. Still pan-handling when I could. Scared because of all of the pending court cases and tickets I'd received. No touching here either.

I had to pay $100 per month for my storage unit. This money came from pan-handling as well. I went to my storage one day and there was a weird brown, liquid substance slowly dripping from the unit above me. I called the fire department because the main office was closed. They put me out because they had to pay a bill to the county because I'd called. Crazy. Needless to say I moved to another storage facility. This is where my soror saved the day with her SUV.

I recall sleeping on one man's sofa near the laundromat. He was friendly. I sat watching TV and he sat; on the other sofa. He asked if I would be uncomfortable if he came and sat next to me. I said yes. That was the last night I spent on his sofa.

It's too bad I didn't have the numbers of all the women I knew who were looking for available men. Are you wondering yet, where are all of the Christian women when a Christian sister needs help?

No I did not sleep with this man either. But after leaving me outside, and knowing that the only people offering me shelter were strange men; why not ask me if, he poisoned my drink. Ask me if he purposely slammed my hand in the door. Ask me if he tied me to a lamp post and threw baseballs at me. Like you really care. You're obviously asking so that you can point at me and say, nannie, nannie boo-boo; either way.

Whether you believe that my life is just a series of unfortunate events (that you, the reader, helped to orchestrate) or you live by the philosophy that a person's life choices make them who they are; either way, human beings weren't meant to live outside (or on the ground) with bugs and animals.

It was completely insane for everyone to leave me outside. They refused to pick me up or socialize with me at all. Police gave me citations to stop me from standing on the median. Only strange men offered me a ride or a spare room to sleep, temporarily. This went on long enough for me to save $5,000. It didn't last of course, we lived off of that money. I sat the 'money for the day', on the night-stand but the rest eventually went into my safe. No there is no money left. (Everyone thinks I'm Letty because she's wearing my black leather mini-skirt, as well! *Fast and Furious*) First and foremost, the money went to hotel costs. Food, when food stamps had run-out. Clothing and shoes for a growing little girl. The money allowed us to keep our clothing clean, it kept me out of the extreme weather; and gave me a chance to rest when I didn't feel well.

It also enabled me and my daughter to take a cab 'to and fro' many times when the bus wasn't an option; and when we couldn't get anyone to give us a ride. ("Well why don't you have a car"? I'll tell you later.) Like getting to my daughter's pediatrician across town. Not to mention my phobias and issues riding the bus during rush-hour. (I was seen asking someone for $4, on the hotel property. In an attempt to get a room one night. I was consequently banned from staying at Motel 6). Our hotel room from then on, was $100 per night at a much nicer hotel. (Thank God, the ban from Motel 6 has been recently lifted.) There were at least 20 – 30 different men at this point, who have either paid for my hotel room or I've slept on their sofa or in their spare room. No I did not sleep with any of them or suck their dicks. Looking back, they must have been reporting in to someone, as to whether or not I slept with them. (Those attempting to sabotage me and embarrass my daughter, are now mad because I'm not ho-ing)."Leave her out there until she starts ho-ing." (If only Dr. King could only hear this). Well I guess the masses were disappointed that this behavior wasn't making their accusations true. So here comes the first wave of sabotage. (At that time, I didn't know).

While my daughter was still living at the same address of the first family member who took us in; (I was unable to stay there; due to no fault of my own); I ended up staying with my cousin, her fiancee' and their two children. (The house I'd driven past while riding with the Federal Police Officer). She had already taken in, my other cousin and her boyfriend from Jersey. Her fiancée' and her two children lived there with her. She was the only one working. Everybody else was looking for a job. It was literally of like living in a roach motel. I was ready to go sleep outside. I was talking on the phone regularly with a guy I'd met at the front desk of a hotel. He was foreign. He was kind enough to come outside and sit on the bench with me when I was out there. He bought me food and we talked for hours. He said he lived with his extended family and couldn't invite me there. (I didn't want him to lose his job by giving a homeless person his hotel discount.) Now if he had a girlfriend or wife, why didn't she come outside to sit with me as well? I'm not saying this because I'm naïve. This was intentional sabotage by anyone who could have picked me and my daughter up and given us refuge together near her school. They knew.

Back in the house. My cousin's boyfriend (from Jersey) invited me to go to the movies. No I didn't go. My working cousin's fiancée's friend, came over to watch a movie with me. Nothing happened. He was very cute. He seemed very nice. He asked me if I wanted to go somewhere. It was mid-nite. I wasn't going anywhere that late with someone I barely knew; not if I'm safely sitting inside the house. I told him that I wanted to go see if I can ride through a tunnel. I have family in the Virginia Beach/Newport area. (I was really just sort of talking to myself). I wanted to move down near my family in the south. (I don't ride through tunnels anymore). Soon the movie went off and I went to sleep. (After he left of course). No kisses, no touching.

On a separate day, I heard one of his other friends who stopped by say, why isn't she throwing herself at me? I'm wondering if he didn't ask sarcastically because of the comment that the actor/actress made about the female spider eating the male spider after sex and him not being a happy meal. That was his name. *Deliver Us From Eva*. Then one evening I watched a movie with my cousins fiancee'; I rarely saw her. When she returned home from work, she went straight to her room and stayed there, just like every other woman I stayed with during this homeless situation. (Married or not). And the ones who didn't stay in their rooms, never invited me to go out with them as a friend. He proceeded to say, she doesn't care what you do. I didn't even ask what he meant. I just kept watching the movie. Then I went to bed; alone. Nothing happened between us.

(I recall sitting outside at Starbucks playing scrabble by myself one homeless afternoon). When I spoke with my foreign friend of 5 months, I told him I wanted to go out. He came to pick me up and I grabbed my Scrabble game. As I got into the car, I said, let's go to the new Harbor. He had this weird look on his face. Where are we going, I said? He drove up to a hotel. I wasn't going to say take me back, I'd finally gotten away from the roaches. I could not believe he brought me to a hotel. Maybe he didn't have any money and was able to get a free room. Then I heard him say as he seemed to whine and hide his face. "You're a ho"-(right)? Wrong. He seemed so nice. All I could think was, that's interesting. So the plot thickens, I thought to myself. Poor thing. He's crazy and nuts just like everybody else. No I'd never seen his penis and he was very short. This was not a sex-thang. The author of this book, is not the crazy one. I had on a sun-dress but I also had my scrabble game as I entered the hotel. Now, how am I the dumb, whore-minded person in this situation? You are all dumb and mean as hell! It was obvious that this was the type of situation that every woman in my circle wanted for me. I figured that after a few of these situations, I wouldn't be homeless anymore and I was correct. Think about what I'm saying. Now we have justification to verbally harass her and call her a ho. The people who have made movies that made me seem less than virtuous, are happy to read situations like the latter. Unbelievable. I would never say, "Let's Be Friends with Benefits".

Anyway, moving on...

I guess when I told her fiancée's' friend I wanted to see if I could ride through a tunnel he told them what I said. I wasn't talking about moving to her sister's house in the north but soon that was the only place I was able to stay. I believe her mother sold the house. Everyone had to leave. I reluctantly left my daughter here at my aunt's with the understanding that she would join me when school ended. (She was still in the home of the first family member who took us in when we became homeless; in Upper Marlboro). I don't understand why, but it didn't work out up north. I won't tell the story, because you won't believe me. There was a really big misunderstanding. I'm glad I was able to help watch their children for a little while. It was summer time. I went back to my bench outside. I never meant to hurt anyone and I pray that their intention wasn't to hurt me. Because I'm not a ho. There and back, I had to ride through a tunnel. I did ok. God was holding me in his arms. Note: No I do not ride through tunnels.

Back on my neck of the woods:

I sat inside IHOP eating and drinking just a bit. They weren't really anxious for me to leave. Helping me find a stable place to live with my daughter or giving me a lead for a job, was out of the question. Well, God showed up once again.

Me and my daughter were invited by an ex-military guy, to stay on base in the Presidential Inn for an entire month. The base where the President of the United States left to go on business trips. I never thought to walk her to the bus-stop. I woke up early **every day** to get or make, her breakfast. She didn't really like having to walk across the entire base to get to the bus-stop outside of the gate, so sometimes she would spend the night at a friend's house. Well, I wasn't interested in the man who invited us nor did I sleep with him, so soon it was off the base and back to the regular hotel for us.

While separated from me, my daughter met a very cute seemingly nice, homeless boy. He used to be in a gang. His father and brother were both in jail. His mother put him out and he had a few black, rotten teeth. He seemed genuine and kind. I finally understand what people mean when they say, you become a product of your environment. No child wants to be in a gang. Yes I make mistakes and don't always say the right thing; but hopefully he knows I care about him. He now also knows what it's like to have a parent wake early every morning to make your breakfast. Long story short; she left the hotel with me to stay with a girlfriend whose mom drove them to school so she could be on time for the last two months of that school year; he ended up living at the girlfriend's house too. No I did not know! I let him stay with us for the last two years of her high school career. They were in love. (I wanted her near me. Not in the street with him). She had a baby. He fell more in love. She graduated and began work and college as he worked at the carwash. He doesn't have a diploma; just a GED. She saw his raging temper one day, and I hadn't met his mother- until the court date when my daughter filed a stay away order. I thought his mother was a drug addict or something. (He said, she tries to use his social security number to get money from his disability and she's violent toward him). I understand she has a house; yet he's not allowed to live in it. No one in his family will let him live with them. He was literally in tears about not having a place to live. OK so my daughter does have a way of provoking the heck out of you. But where are all of the black men out here? We need some big brother programs for young men like him. He needs to rent a room in a safe peaceful environment so that he can learn the right way to do things. He is now renting a room in a very unsafe environment. We all learn from our mistakes. Life goes on. He's turning his life around. He's never smoked or done drugs and he's a very hard worker. He's taking care of his kid financially. (He comes to see him quite often). Minimum wage really needs to be at least $12 per hour in every state; truly. My daughter has a child now. Hopefully now she'll focus on school, not boys. My daughter told me that they are no longer together and they won't be in the future. I can't say that I blame her for wanting to have a baby while she had a man by her side who also wanted a baby; even though I would have preferred that she be married. The sad part is that so many times Blacks have to have children in order to get a job or to get money from the state just to survive.

Given the track record of the woman that she's met and the family she sees on a regular basis, marriage isn't certain and old age will creep up on you. There are way too many single women who haven't had children in our (former) social circle. And the other women she met, left us homeless too long. "Oh, they're not ho's either"? No they're not. The longer you wait, I guess the greater the chance of you catching one of these deadly diseases.

Chapter 2

In Need Of Income

When I first returned home during my separation from my husband, I was halfway through hair school and needed to find a job on this end to continue paying my tuition. I applied to Circuit City, which only made sense with a Mass Communications Degree. I would have been able to keep up with technology. I was not hired. However, I received employment at Home Depot. I swear; I was being set-up for failure, even then. I finished school, passed the exam and began worked in the Cosmetology field. I never received the support I needed to make it my one and only career. Then I began trying to find any job that would allow me and my daughter to live independently. That's where life began to get tricky. Money was so tight that I never even thought about trying to break into the field I'd gone to college to pursue. My focus was my daughter. I lived in an area where I did not want her to go to the public school. My brother went to school around in that same complex before I'd begun school. He had a terrible experience; way back then.

I remember once, when I'd first became homeless I'd gone down to the train station and stood up in front of all of the rows of chairs and commanded everyone's attention. I made them aware that I was homeless and explained how I'd lost my job. Then I asked if they could spare a dollar. (Well, it didn't really work out the way I thought it would). I did get a few bucks though.

Have you ever seen a homeless person and wondered how they ended up that way? Have you ever stopped for a minute to actually ask them? I know, life moves too fast to be bothered with such issues. Plus, they might be dangerous.

What if you stopped briefly to speak to a homeless person and he or she told you about a series of unfortunate events. What if they told you that they had been trying to work but every time they are hired, the staff on each job harassed them and sabotaged their work? I don't care if they used to be an alcoholic or a prostitute; harassing them when they re-enter working society is truly insane. I know, you believe homeless people are all paranoid. Even if you stop to listen, you probably won't stop to listen for 10 whole minutes. People tend to equate homelessness with addictions, unfortunately. So if you stutter because you're hurt, you get 15 seconds, tops. No, I've never been an alcoholic nor a prostitute, yet I've been harassed on every job I've accepted since I've become homeless (and a few times before); so much so that I am unable to work. Everybody does not have money and a credit card to relocate. In their defense, please allow me to share my own encounter with such a challenge.

Wal-mart was making its debut into the nation's capital. Everyone was excited. I figured this could be a chance for me to work, free from harassment as the neighborhood homeless lady. I'd never lived or pan-handled in D.C. I applied and was offered an interview. I was offered full-time employment and asked to return for what they termed, a hiring interview. On the same date of my second interview with Wal-Mart, I'd scheduled an interview for earlier that day, with a restaurant that also had not had its grand opening yet. I'd planned to work at Wal-Mart full-time and part-time at the restaurant. I'd expressed that I had another interview and had to leave at a certain time. As my interview with the restaurant came to an end, the interviewer said out loud, make that job, part-time. I planned to do nothing of the sort. I just ignored him and left; deciding that this wasn't the job for me. Once I arrived at Wal-Mart, my hire date was confirmed and I began to fill-out paperwork. Part-time, it read. Why does it say part-time, I asked? She said they would change it later. I couldn't believe it. It was as if the man from the restaurant had called. It really wasn't worth the trip to travel so far for a part-time job. I accepted the position and tried to make it work. Long story made short: I was being verbally harassed by my immediate, black, male supervisor; I was being followed by his white, male supervisor and I was being stalked and hit-on by the cutest guy in the store. Everyone kept saying; he's taken. I didn't care, he was coming on to me. He was the only one in the entire store trying to be my friend. I asked if he had a girlfriend and he said no. I just wanted to be cordial without getting into a love triangle. Bottom line, I ended up leaving due to extended travel time and harassment. I worked there for several months around a couple of extremely smelly but very friendly guys. They all lied and said I smelled. It was unbelievable.

There are many different smells around us every day. If someone walks to their job from the subway station, he or she may smell like the outdoors when they enter a building. Spraying a light scent on your clothing or just letting time go by, usually solves such an issue. Now when someone comes indoors and he or she smells like urine or defecation, that's a different issue.

This was not the only job that I held during my time of homelessness. It was an intentional, rigorous effort to create a pattern on my resume that suggests that I can't keep a job, when I attempted to work while "homeless". I was clearly being harassed. Before I became homeless, there were legitimate reasons for switching jobs. My daughters age and my need to create my own hours, was one reason. I left the cosmetology field to focus on a career with a more stable income. Sometimes realizing that choice was not going to work-out for me. Because it had been easy to work in cosmetology, I returned to work in that field with different areas of expertise; like esthetics or make-up. My need to focus on a part-time job while working my full-time job, was another reason. I also worked a summer job when the school year was out, during the 7 years I worked for the school system.

Now remember, by this time, I'm traumatized. You can't tell by looking at me but I am. I was contingently hired by UPS and Metro Access, which were both excellent paying jobs. I couldn't continue the hiring process with either company because I don't ride elevators nor can I ride in the back of the training van for routine training runs. You would think that all of the letters I'd written about my situation and the fact that the entire community knew I was homeless, would have caused the managers in either company to place me in another position. They knew I had a Communications Degree. Dispatch would have been perfect.

When I say I can't work, I'm not being lazy. I told you, you wouldn't believe me. I do not sell sex, nor did I used to.

Well I thank God that I'm not sleeping outside today but who knows where I'll be tomorrow with this strange group of earthlings I live amongst. (And I, not my daughter, did sleep outside for what would be equivalent to about a week adding up those particular days.) I wrote every politician, law official, foreign embassy (in the nation's capital) and church pastor you could think of; more than once. Everyone was now aware that even though they believed I would sell sex if left homeless, we will have major problems if I couldn't get money by other means. (I admit, a few of my letters may have been confusing and/or unprofessionally written. I was so angry, hurt and tired).

You are all going out of your way to tell me that no man wants me. I do not care if no man wants to marry me. Frankly, anyone who uses the word ho in the way that you all do, is beneath me and we would never need to be in a relationship anyway. My poor, poor former Black slave 'brotheren' and 'sisteren'.

Even though it would have been more appropriate when my daughter was in grade school; I still desire to support her financially and she still needs my help. That is another reason why I'm writing this book. I'm also looking for people to interview so that I can build a portfolio of writing samples. Even if you don't believe I would make it as a writer, why not grant me an interview? That's why I believe that the excuses that you all make and names you call me are just an attempt to keep me poor and in a lower position than yourself because you're insecure.

Make Her Appear To Be Selling Sex

{I had one hand in my pocket; the other ones holding a homeless sign. (You would think they were psychic.) I was living in a hotel not far from the military base. I purchased groceries for my daughter and took them to her. Unfortunately the only people who offered to give me a ride to take them to her, were men whom I did not know. They were all super nice. These weren't the men who offered the spare rooms, these were different men who I spoke with once I got outside and began to pan-handle that particular day. They didn't even ask for gas money. It was still a very unfortunate situation. I'm sure it was enough for them to just aide in the process of making the on-looker believe that I was a prostitute.}

I'm not sure if I was banned from the shopping center where I pan-handled because I was there so long, every day, or because this young man began practically stalking me in his attempt to offer me a place to rest. (Sabotage like what I'm about to share with you, lead the police to believe that I was a prostitute and they ultimately stopped me from pan-handling; at least temporarily until I wrote the chief and clarified the matter).

A very attractive young man, aged 22, has pulled his car up to me at least 4 different times within a 6 month period to tell me about the basketball camp he was starting. (I played basketball from age 10 til age 20). There was obviously a large number of people who wanted to convince those watching, that I was a prostitute. One day he offers me a chance to relax out of the heat with him at his parent's home not far from the shopping mall where I was actually pan-handling. One afternoon, I went with him and I watched television then took a short nap; alone; on a twin bed in a spare room. No I did not have sex with him. I didn't see him again until about a month or so later when I was **literally sitting outside at the local laundromat**, at night fall, thanking God that I was not the type of person who would intentionally leave someone outside; (*Columbiana*) and (*The Blind Side* – What a coincidence, the police officer who lives two houses over from the house where I lived all of my life, shares the name of the boy in this movie). Pan-handling is against the law. What a predicament to be in. You know it's ironic that the old-timer mustang she's driving sure looks a lot like the one our (life-long) next door neighbors had stolen from them at the mall not far from here, many years ago. I also find it ironic that the same car was stolen in the movie, *Getting There*. I bet you didn't know that the twin star in this movie who only has one first name (in real life), shares the name of my first loves, younger sister.

Here again, he pulls up to me; but this time he offered me shelter for the evening. (Note: he has the same name as the little boy in Florida who was shot by the neighborhood watch guy). He drove me a little farther away this time to his grandmother's house. (It must be God who's kept me from being chopped up and stuffed in a trunk somewhere). It was not clean enough to sleep on the floor and there was no sofa in the living room. There was someone else sleeping in the other bedroom. I couldn't sleep in his grandmother's room. No I did not have sex with him but why would everyone I know, do something so cruel. His grandmother was out of town for 3 days so I was able to stay until she returned. It was not my desire to live with men, strange or familiar. I can't believe everyone was trying to set me up for failure. I do not desire to be a part of his basketball camp or anything else that he may organize. I wish him well. No I was not going to suck his dick or sleep with him to get a job. Although I was very attracted to him. Hopefully he will be able to transform the lives of hundreds of talented young boys.

I have never laid on my back and let a man insert his penis into my vagina for employment or for a place to rest my head. It doesn't matter if you believe me. I wake up with myself every day; in this regard I'm just fine.

At this point everyone wants to offer me lunch. Hop in. Let's go eat. All homeless people are hungry right? Not when everybody wants you to get in there car to go eat! Most of the time there would be an offer from someone whom seemed trust worthy. I usually didn't stop pan-handling to go eat because I could buy my own food. But sometimes a conversation was appreciated. (I had to become a potential missing person just to stimulate my brain). A ride was great in the evening, heading to my hotel, a lot of times, because I have claustrophobic issues on over-crowded buses during rush-hour.

Chapter 3

I Didn't Give In and I Lost a Friend

The following relationships mentioned where close friendships that I'd developed with men and believe it or not, one woman; throughout the years, where each of them attempted to get me to fall sexually. (And no I didn't play with their penises or perform oral sex). I didn't give in and the friendship ultimately dissolved. There have been more, but I thought I would share these few.

I had a lot of pictures of me and my basketball team-mate and best friend from high school, all over my dorm wall in college. She wasn't my best friend because we went to the movies a lot or because we ate out a lot (we had busy lives). She was my best friend because I liked being around her; we had things in common. I thought we made each other better people. That doesn't seem to be the case any longer). Still, it's very important to do things together in between the 'busyness'. (Today, we're no longer friends.) Maybe people wanted to see my wall to decide if I was gay or not. (There weren't any pictures of a boyfriend on the wall).

Now when her father drove her to college, I went too. It seemed as if a lot of my friends went south, especially to Hampton. Guess who else went there, initially? My green-eyed friend. I stopped past his dorm room as he was unpacking. No he didn't try to kiss me or anything. Now does that mean he didn't like me or does that mean he's a gentleman?

"We'd already kissed, back home." I'd leaned over and kissed him. Months before I spent prom night, lying next to him, on the floor in his home, in front of the TV; fully clothed. It was great. The kiss and Prom Night. Too bad I was headed for college in the opposite direction. I cried as we rode back north and left her at her new home away from home.

When I was in college I was very out-going and friendly. Most blacks spoke as they passed each other. Maybe because it was a white school. On 5 separate occasions during my freshman year, there was a male friend in my dorm room and I was very fond of them all. Pay very close attention to what I'm saying. First, I must say that I do not always act on my feelings. Secondly, I must say, I can tell when a guy is trying to get me to see that he is interested. Lastly, I can usually tell if they don't really think I'm cute enough. The first person I'll mention is my boyfriend from home who drove me to school, during the time when we were in a relationship; (not my first love). One was a potential boyfriend in college whom I was getting to know. We kissed and necked and stuff. Did we go to the movies? No. Did we go to the harbor? No. Did we go eat off campus? No.

Now, let me take a moment to explain to the ghetto person who says, "You were ho-ing"; and to the educated person who says," You were pressed." You are both wrong. If I was just a ho to him, why was he devastated when I left? No, he didn't have a car. He was from a rural area so he's not used to riding the metro bus. He has fun inside. We had a connection verbal and physical. He really liked me and being with me was enough for him. I really liked him too. Maybe he should have just invited me to go to a Sigma party. Lol. (As a substitute teacher years later, I sat at my desk studying music as my class did their work. I was attempting to teach myself to read music so that I could write a song and not just a poem. Then came the movie, *Drumline*).

Let me just side-track for a moment:

I guess I chose to marry another black man (my only husband so far),

who basically refused to date me too. But we prayed and we worked out together, outdoors. Even after marriage, we never really dated. I left him too. He was devastated too? (We spent our time at church). My cousin has never been to college, never been married and has no children. She's my age. (Many other woman can identify with her). This particular cousin was one of my many bridesmaids. And I invited her on a road trip with me and my daughter to Miami. Her father was a chef, she's a great cook, she's working and she has big titty's. So what's been the problem all this time? But I bet she has a man right now; and I do not. I'm sorry; I just don't think it's the women. Now the world will be aware that I'm the Global ho and not her; she may actually have a fighting chance- (Sarcasm). Oh, maybe she's the octopus in the Little Mermaid; she does have a lot of gray hair. Her voice is very high pitched. (She'd probably make a great singer). Maybe I'll just sell all of the belongings in my storage, buy a car and become a vehicular nomad. (Since I have 20 very small, cork-crew whatchamagigems). The guy on the beach, in The Little Mermaid, does share the name of my last 5 year relationship (while I was homeless). And the 7 year relationship that ended last year, had and loves, really big dogs.

I also have another aunt who loves children and hasn't married or had any children. She is a teacher. I suppose she is the star of the TV show, Alice. She shares the name of one of the waitresses. She is tall, very light-skinned with very light brown hair. I guess she is also the spokes-person for Progressive Insurance and the reflection of the blue fish in Finding Nemo.

Back to the original story:

One, was a guy from my class whom which I was studying. All we did was study. He was really cute and really nice. (Note: No one knocked on my door and asked me if I was busy, when I was studying). He looked a lot like Malcolm X. And there were two other guys, both from the New Jersey/New York area. This (set-up), was a completely different time and space during my freshman year. Looking back, I'm not sure if his reason for being too anxious was because his friend mentioned an interest in me first or because his breath was so bad. They were like really close. I thought they were best friends. I actually kissed the one with the terrible breath- (an octopus). Now remember, they came to my room at separate times during the year. The other one whom I was actually more attracted too, was telling me a story from his past regarding a girlfriend who'd died. He never tried to touch me. I guess the sob story was supposed to make me become the aggressor. Now these two guys were something else. They tried everything in the book to get me to sleep with them. Nothing worked. We weren't dating; and no I didn't kiss him. I really liked him but I knew in the back of my mind that he didn't think I was cute enough. (The next day, I saw him walking, holding hands with another girl who was lighter, but shared my name; as if I'd done something wrong-I didn't care). I refused to sleep with either of them. Eventually we spoke again but after I graduated, I had never heard from them again. OK, it was like a quest to try to get me to fall. Maybe, them coming to my room, gave the wrong appearance and caused my sorors to believe that I wasn't a true Christian? This is the crazy twist. It's been almost 20 years, and the girl I saw him walking with pulled up to me at Starbucks last month and we spoke briefly. (I was pan-handling). Come to find out, she is still best friends with my soror. The one who pledged me to ANQ. She was trying to be sarcastic and mean toward me. What did I do? People are just nuts. I'm not a liar and I'm not a ho. If you like me; invite me out. Don't kiss me passionately, hoping that I get weak and have sex with you. I don't have sex casually nor do I kiss casually. They didn't change their minds because I smelled. I said no.

Just for a moment travel back with me to campus:

This (second set-up), is a story that you'll hear from the guys down here in my city, probably told to the masses by the guy left sitting on the bed. This tall, dark, gorgeous guy with the locks, who has a name straight from the bible, knocked on my dorm door while the guy that I told you about; that I was to getting to know, was trying hard to get in my pants.

(We were close).

He had been hurt by a former girlfriend, (he mentioned it every time we were together). We did things outside together but it seemed more important to him to 'lay up under me'. I really did like him a lot. When I opened the door, this other guy asked if I was busy and I said no. Let's go, he said. I left. We walked and talked. I left the other guy sitting right on my bed. I would much rather not be lead into a fornicating situation. I guess I didn't handle it very well but I didn't care. Now, this guy that I left sitting on my bed walked up to me about 6 months ago at 7-eleven while I was pan-handling and said I will not be anybody's girlfriend now.

Even when he's being mean to me or not making a lot of sense; I think he's very attractive. I really liked him when we were in school. It can never be my loss if you're trying to make me fall. I may be alone, but I'm true to myself. And I wake up every day, thankful and happy that I know God.

I just looked at him and kindly said hello and then good-bye. At this same time, at the same place, my first love's stepfather walked up to me and said, yeah, you gone be short..........I just simply thought to myself, "I thank God for Jesus".

Now the guy that I told you who had given me a ride to school, invited me back to his home. We were no longer together as boyfriend and girlfriend but our parents worked together. That's what I told people when they asked how we met, (our parents worked together). I simply sat on the sofa listening. (He broke-up with me some time prior to my visit). He knew he had broken my heart. He leaned over and put a 'hicky' on my neck. He didn't touch me with his hands at all. I hadn't had a 'hicky' on my neck since middle school; if ever. And I wasn't having sex then. I couldn't believe it. But it didn't really matter, I didn't have a boyfriend. I just shook my head. When I returned to campus, the guy who saved me from the clutches of the rabid octopus (with the bad breath) -did I say octopus; I mean, squid; the cry-baby whose heart had been broken before arriving at Towson and the curious perpetrator who told a sob story of an ex-girlfriend dying; who already had a special girl on campus; said he didn't trust me anymore because he saw a 'hicky' on my neck. Nothing happened. He didn't even touch me with his hands. I was just sitting there. I didn't think about why he invited me until this very moment of writing this book – He never said put in a good word with your mother. His mother worked for my mother and he'd broken my heart. I want my grandchildren to know the truth. (I wasn't naked when I said no to any of these guys). "Talk about being set-up straight out the gate". I didn't sleep with any of them except for my boyfriend from home who dropped me off. He was commuting from home, taking classes at a college nearby. And none of these situations were back to back. Just friends attempting to take it further. This was not going on while I was in a relationship with my boyfriend.

(And no I wasn't giving out blow-jobs. I didn't even know that giving blow-jobs was a thing; until well after my marriage had ended.)

I'm not bi-sexual or gay. I do not cheat in relationships but everyone believes I do. I'm not easy and the guy I left sitting there on my dorm bed, did not have a small penis nor was he ugly. (He opened his pants).

I guess you can understand that between the dorm noise of my freshmen neighbors and the distracting visits from male friends, who knew I was kind and sweet or were maybe obsessed with my TV character, blossom; why I wanted to move off campus. Yeah I wore her hat, we had the same nose and I was soon to be given, Blossom as a nick-name on campus (not by everyone). I'm not a ho and I don't sell sex. (This is just college. Why would a man want to marry a woman who is constantly tormented by mirrored images of herself on television, so much so that she is questioned at work or at school? How would she ever work and take care of herself and her family?)

Well, there was a specific group of freshman that I hung with (male and female). We did a lot of fun things together. I was actually attracted to 3 of the 4 guys we hung out with but none of them showed any interest in me. The one I really liked gave me the name Blossom and must have been comparing me to the show because every now and then he would give me these disapproving looks. I didn't even really watch the show that much. I also knew he had feelings for one particular girl in our group. Once we had a party in my dorm room. Me and the girl he had a crush on, shared the same birthday. (Her best friend, who was in our little group too, had the same name as Shaire's best friend in *Clueless*). Quite a few people came. The pictures make it seem wilder than it was. There were bottles but I didn't drink, any. (No, I didn't kiss or sleep with any of them.) And they were all cute. The guys had formed a basketball squad for intramural and so had we young women. (Including my roommate). One day before a game, I stopped and ate a meal from Burger King. Didn't think anything of it. During the middle of the game, I began to itch severely. Iran out of the gym, pulling off clothing. Shortly after, the girls were in the rest room with me. I had hives everywhere. I'd lost my sight and they were all yelling, praying and calling the ambulance and my mother. I knew I was having an allergic reaction. I just didn't know why. The EMS people stuck something in my arm and my vision came back just in time for me to see bloodshot straight up in the air. I was now in the emergency room. Benadryl, oxygen and an I V saved my life. (And a lot of caring people). I survived. My mother and father managed to make it to me in one piece even though she did 90 miles per hour down the high-way to get to me. The next day I went back to Burger King to see what may have caused this. They had cooked my fries in the same grease as the monthly special; shrimp. Yes, I knew I was allergic to seafood. I'd had one episode like this before after having dinner with my parents and going walking at the track. The second incident was a lot worse.

(When I moved off campus I guess they figured I was out of the way so they could all get 'bunned' up and forget about me. Not one visit from any of them; ever).

If you think about it, it seemed as if the guys from my area were sent there just to keep those women from becoming my friend. They were like draped over these girls like lava. The men from the New York/New

Jersey area (where they make movies), seemed to be sent to Towson just to try to make me lose my focus.

Speaking of being all 'bunned' up. In the movie, "Getting Even With Dad", a promotions department project during my internship at an Advertising Agency.; it sure seems pretty obvious that the actors are trying to get someone to eat a hot dog and take some medicine-Nike's slogan makes a quick cameo appearance, reminding you of its motto; 'just do it'. The campaign began the first year I became intimate with my first love -1988. No I did not perform oral sex; nor did I begin then. This movie debuted when I was interning at an advertising agency during college. So my brother usually catches the bus when traveling. I guess you can say he is estranged from my father because he is the one who said he had to leave because he wasn't being productive. We didn't argue with our parents and my father didn't throw things around the house; especially a plant; like the scenes in this movie. Now, it seems as if the cast of *Why Did I Get Married*, are trying to show you (for the second time) who actually threw the plant. Even though it's not actually clear who threw it, they've decided to use the names of our family member who actually wears scrubs to work; lost her only son to violence, and probably argues sometimes with her husband because he is a wounded veteran and has been traumatized and drinks. (Very similar to the scenes in this movie).

Anyway; let's focus on campus once again:

I was usually able to get a ride home with another friend of mine from my area. He had a girlfriend and nothing happened between us. He had the same name as my cousin who moved away to Chicago. From what I understand, my cousin worked for Obama when he was a senator. He still lives there with his wife and three children. He had a different mom than his brothers. His brother is the one who struck me while in my aunt's home with my daughter. "Well, what's his name?" You wonder. You know the boy with the frog, in Cheaper By the Dozen; that's his name. And we love him dearly. His wife shares my name.

Another male, freshman friend or mine on campus was the third-string quarter back. He was nice. (He drove a hot-red Prelude). After getting to know me, he decided that it would be a good idea for me to meet one of his fellow team-mates who spoke of Jesus, just as much as I did. He came to my room and we spoke right at the entrance of my room. We never even sat down. We talked, we prayed, I think we kissed good-bye and we both knew. He was the one. I was the one. But he was busy and I was busy; so we both went on our way. We talked quite often after that; at first.

Now I still had males (who were already my friends), show interest in me off campus in my new apartment, but it was different. I had my car with me and I was seeing my soon to be husband (although he was hardly around). I remember my ex (hicky) asking me why I was trusting that my soon to be husband was being faithful to me, traveling around with the Redskins practice football squad. He wanted us to get back together. I said no. Now why not just invite me out as a friend? He didn't have to try to convince me to invite him to my apartment and to not trust my soon to be husband while he was away. Instead of inviting me back to his home for a hicky; invite me to go somewhere nice. He never thought of that huh? Well, I'm not going to think of it for him. I'm going to talk to whomever I want. I'm not a ho, he's just a black man who probably took advantage of a lot of women before he decided to settle down. I guess he was trying to tell me that my soon to be husbands family, was from the inner-city and he wasn't. Or maybe Hollywood called and he was aware that I was being cheated on. Whichever the reason; my husband had family and friends on set in Hollywood.

I'd never thrown a party in this apartment. Never bought or drank alcohol. Never smoked anything in there either. And never had a visit from any Christian sorors. We had plenty of gathering that I attended; including the Sunday service we held in the Susquehanna room.

These first two guys who came to visit me, were close friends of mine. One was a friend from high school who came to visit and the other was a friend from college who came by to hang out. Neither suggested that we go out anywhere but they both, on different days of course, wanted to hang out in my apartment with me. I didn't kiss or sleep with either one of them.(I'm not saying this because I feel guilty, I'm saying this because you need to get a clear understanding of what I'm saying. I read the bible with the guy who works in the government now. My friend from high school was just sitting around in my room as if he was waiting for me to maybe, kiss him. Just too weird. I ended up answering my phone and talking to someone else while he was there. They were both very cute, nice and smart. One works for the government now and one is a minister.

I had traveled to Hampton University where I was visiting several girlfriends during what I believe was homecoming week. I knew a lot, of both men and women from my area who were attending that particular school at that time. I ran into an old friend from a nearby neighborhood back home. He was one of the nicer guys from the Boys and Girls Club. We were walking on campus and he invited me and my friend to come off campus to hang out with him and his friend from home. We watched TV talked about old times and everything that was going on with everyone in college. He invited me to see his room, around the corner as my friend and his friend, sat in the living room. He kissed me. I stopped him from taking it any further and shortly after, things felt weird. He and I returned to the living room. He soon took us back to campus to her dorm room. I'm not going to tell you that he shares the same name as the dog; on, *Dog with a Blog*. (My green-eyed friend had transferred to another college in North Carolina).

Then there was 'the super-model' octopus who was an old friend from the Boys and Girls Club, whom I'd invited over to my apartment shortly after I'd separated from my husband. For some reason he was very clutchy. He was very attractive though. I know that a lot of women would kill to be with him so he's not used to being turned down when it comes to sex. I guess I shouldn't have kissed him. But no means no and he had to accept that. Unfortunately he didn't; so I ended up telling him that my ex-husbands grandmother had just died from AIDs and they think I might have it too. He finally left me alone. Well, it was the truth.

During my brief employment with the phone company, I was invited to my supervisor's home for dinner. Needless to say, I turned him down. (During my eventful *Baby Boy* production). You'll see. Just keep reading.

I was invited to hang-out in Georgetown on three separate occasions. All the dates were after my marriage ended. One with a (former) life-long, (Boys and Girls Club), friend whom had lost his twin brother in a house fire when we were in high school and the second guy whom I'd met, I believe at Wild World Amusement Park. He was actually a mutual friend of my male cousin. Just two relaxing evenings through a beautiful part of DC. No, I didn't smell and from what I could recall, nothing strange happened on either date. But there was never a second date. (The surviving twin's mom actually paid for a week at the hotel where me and my daughter were staying, a few years ago; in the midst of our homeless situation). I liked him, and we dated; unheard of!

Well, what about the third guy, you ask. I guess it must have been a coincidence that the woman in Look *Who's Talking Now*; is wearing a red and white poke-a-dot dress with a matching straw hat; (as I wore on the Spirit of Washington Cruise with my parents. But I wore a matching straw hat). She is married to a commercial airplane pilot. Five years after the movie was made I was working as an esthetician at Pentagon City Mall, not far from national Airport. One of my clients was a Caucasian, commercial airplane pilot who reminded me an awful lot, of the knight who saved the day in *Pretty Woman*. We dated; in Georgetown. We danced in a club and went to dinner in a nice restaurant. But he invited me to his home once where we sat on the sofa and he kissed me. He is a big drinker and very aggressive. I am not. I was very uncomfortable; fully clothed. I didn't like that. So I left.

When the holiday season rolled around, I walked through the local mall and I happened to notice exotic pictures of men on a group of calendars that were being displayed at a holiday sells booth. The model and owner of the calendars was a guy who struck up a conversation with me and shared that his family was out of town. He invited me to his apartment to hang out on an upcoming day during the holiday week. That's not usually something I would do with a complete stranger, (unless I'm left homeless), but against my better judgment, I chose to live a little. They weren't naked pictures. My aunt actually has his pictures all over her bedroom. (I didn't notice the pictures in her home until after my date). We talked quite often and he lived in a very nice area on the other side of the bridge. We watched TV, ate dinner and I actually sipped a glass of wine. He tried to get me to disrobe but of course the answer was no. He seemed very surprised. He said I must not be the one for him. I agreed and shortly thereafter, ended up leaving.

I was working at the spa but happened to be standing in the retail part of the store when a young man walked by and caught my eye. The closer he got, the more I realized that he was a woman. She asked about our skincare for men and complemented me on my beautiful smile. She took my breath away. Her approach was so flattering. We talked a lot and dated for a little while. We became close. She invited me to her home to braid her hair and we kissed. She laid on the bed and we stopped the situation before it went too far too soon. We both remained fully clothed; however, I gently grabbed and sucked on both of her double D breast. She ended up moving away to go to school. We spent a lot of time together before she left. I didn't want to take a female relationship any further than that and I told her so. At that moment, I was choosing not to be a lesbian. (During this time I had cut my hair off, 'boy' short, with stud earrings). I remember telling a male friend of mine that I'd kissed a girl and I liked it. He just shook his head with a half-cocked smile.

I recall meeting a man who I struck up a conversation with while at work. I revealed that I was a licensed hair stylist but I wasn't currently in a shop. He asked me, if while his daughter was with him, I would do her hair. He paid me of course. We became friends and he invited me to his cook-out. There were a lot of people there. He was in a historically black, fraternity. On one separate occasion, I visited with him and he gave me a tour of his home. He proceeded to try to get me to lay down with him and I refused. After that our friendship ended. I lost a hair client; his daughter.

I recall having my boyfriend's best buddy to help me move some boxes from my apartment to my storage before I moved to my aunt's. Yes, this is the 7 year on and off relationship I will often speak of. When He and I were done moving stuff, I showered and he was attempting to come in the bathroom, I said, ah no dude. Then I realized it was probably just my man testing me. I washed my hair and got dressed. I then sat on the floor with him and showed him my photo albums. I think he had a run in with the law. I believe he may be in jail right now.

Well, these people are guys who wanted to take things to the next level before I wanted to. I liked these guys. But attempting to pressure me into becoming intimate, then disappearing after I say no; isn't cool. I'm worth befriending. But those who already knew me, should have known that I was worth keeping around as a friend.

It's too bad I didn't have the numbers of all the women I knew who were looking for available men. Lol.

Well I have a cousin whose name is being used in another movie where she and her husband are arguing because their son died. The woman is wearing scrubs. My cousin wears scrubs for her job. Now she stood next to me intentionally, when I was in her home a few years back, brushing her hair frantically; twice. I had no idea why. Now if someone were to read this book, they may think The Pursuit of Happiness and PS I Love You, are about her and her husband. I guess you can't believe everything you read, huh?

The Pursuit of Happiness is about an actual man and his family. He argued with his wife then became homeless with his son. He aspired to be a stock broker. It's not about me or my brother or our family. They used a scene straight from this movie to get viewers to correlate the argument scene and the insane hair brushing scene, with that of the actors in PS I Love You and The Pursuit of Happiness. Even knowing that one is based on a true story, people are hell-bent on believing that it's all about me and my husband. Neither movie is about me and my husband nor my brother. And yes my brother initially aspired to be a stock broker. He's being sabotaged. (Do you think it was a coincidence that my husband found a job quickly at a stock broking library, right out of college? I don't.) Now I've never collected glasses of half drunken juice from each member at the dinner table and poured it back into the container. (That is degusting). I would never discourage anyone's dreams by being sarcastic. But I've also never been one to brush my hair frantically or argue and then have sex to make it better.

Not even in high school when young folks jokingly called each other ho's and bitches; which was extremely rare (on my bus and in my classes) and never directed toward myself; did I find it amusing or appropriate. I'm a grown woman now and many people believe I have a childlike silliness about me. I still find no place for that word in my vocabulary (toward another person), nor do I understand why so many people who consider themselves classy, who have never even held a conversation with me, find it befitting to call me out of my name. **No matter what career field I choose, the harassment is real and so intense that it affects my work. When the harassment doesn't work, then the sabotage begins. Whether I'm cutting hair, teaching children or running a cash register**.

It is my hope that this book will be a major conversation piece before I pass away. There just may be one normal minded person somewhere on this planet who reads this and understands what I'm dealing with. I'm not paranoid. I know for a fact that I'm not crazy. And I do not have body odor issues.

God's ways are so beyond me. He said that he would- that it'd be for my good, so I should just rest and believe. Well if there's one thing that's hard to come by when you're homeless, is rest. This entire situation is so beyond violence and tears. It's almost beyond compensation;

however, purchasing this book would be a definite jolt in the right direction.

Although I'm happy alone, I embraced male companionship because it's only natural. They were my friend's years ago or the only friends I was allowed to have, later in life; when I was left homeless. Clearly, I wasn't having sex with them just because they were my life-long friends. Although, I was always hoping for the best. Maybe an invite for a date, after a kiss; that did not result in a sexual experience. I'm sorry. Blacks are pathetic. My tears are probably not falling for the reason that you believe.

More than anything, I want to use my talents and enjoy my life with female friends, cousins my age, male friends and male intimate partners. Why wouldn't this be want I want?

A Few Mistakes, a Heap of Rumors and a Sentence of Homelessness

I'm sure the greatest rumor by far is the one that I don't know about. Something in a movie that I've not seen. I will never know that everyone believes this particular lie, about me. That is why it's so easy for me to be happy alone.

The lies that are believed, are why the rumors begin and how sabotage is able to fester. Yes I'm a grandmother and I carry an umbrella everywhere when I pan-handle. My grandchild's name is not Nina and I do not have a bladder control issue. However, my daughter has a thing about using public rest-rooms. She holds her water. She has just been diagnosed with a bladder infection. *Nina Has To go*.

Now I played basketball in high school but accepting the courtship of a boy who wanted to be my boyfriend, was never an issue. And I usually broke up with them. I just can't believe that I'm 40 years old and my man just met me 5 years or so ago and all this time, he and probably the entire world, believes that the *Rebound* movie is about me. The smelters was the name of the team. (The smelled hers). I've watched the movie once or twice before and never even gave it a second thought because I know that was never an issue. I guess playing basketball really was like social suicide.

A rumor that I just can't seem to shake, is that I slept with a man who was my best friend, then I refused to marry him. Now this so called best friend was the first person that made me realize the 'one friend at a time rule,' that was now in effect. **There was a one-friend at a time rule; and a, I can only go to the movies or bowling or to a cook-out with someone that I'm not attracted to; rule.** All at once, I had no one; no friends what so ever, and he was the only person left talking to me in the entire community; for some strange reason. Could it have been because he looked just like the short, fat, chocolate man in Brown Sugar who sang,"The ho is mine"?....... Although it was his desire; no I did not marry him.

We had been friends since we were in middle school. I'd been knowing of him before that; in the Boys and Girls club. Now if you find it wrong that I did this, then, why would it be OK for any man to do this to me? I'm saying that I didn't sleep with him. I don't lead people on. But If I allow him to take me on 10 dates then say, "I'm not interested." Would that be wrong? I make it clear from the beginning if I can sense that a guy likes me and I don't feel the same way. Many years ago, before I began college; his mother helped me get a summer job at the State Department. He used to work there too. He didn't go off to college. He now works as a car salesman. He's married with children.

I have a project for you. See how many adult and kid movies you can find that have a character named Ellie. I was working for the Department of Defense on Fort Myer another summer before I began college. I mispronounced ELLE magazine. I said Ellie. (Legally Blonde told you; any Cosmopolitan girl would know). The girl working next to me in my office looked at me like I was from Mars.

(As I sit here, babysitting my grandson, I saw a commercial for a babysitting site called Care.com. The little girl said her stuffed dog; Armstrong; makes a great co-pilot but he's not such a good babysitter. The babysitter they chose from the list, was named Ellie). Unbelievable.

Well, now I have a cosmetology license so I try to stay 'In The Know'.

I was very hurt by the children verbally harassing me out of my teaching career. Devastated after losing my job; with tears in my eyes, I just drove my brand new Camry back to the dealer and left it there. (I had not bought my car from my car salesman friend. I felt like I would be taking advantage of him). I didn't think about selling it or anything. When the smoke cleared; (what smoke, you ask?); the smoke pouring out of my ears. I laid on the floor in the cake-pan room at my aunt's house, absolutely numb. I may not make as much money as a doctor or an attorney but I loved to teach. I cared about them. They provoked me and didn't want me to succeed. A student from a High School class where I'd previously taught, told me they were trying to make me lose my job. It still brings tears to my eyes when I think about it. All of the lies. I didn't have one complaint of any kind regarding the way I smelled, for seven years in the school system. Not from a student, a parent, a co-worker or an administrator. But the day I lost my job, a student yelled out, "Because it smells"; out of nowhere. I lost my job because I smacked a large male student on the arm after he knocked me over while he was fighting another male student. All of this happened in one day. Now I "smell" and I'm "violent".

I now have asthma from writing on the chalk boards before dry-erase boards were put in every class-room. But just like my unemployment, my workers compensation was denied.

I know of a principal who punched a student in the face while breaking up a fight. He lost his job but parents in the nation's capital and I suppose some teachers, rallied and he got this job back.

Let me give you an example of how this childish rumor has become way out of control. As I stood on a small median on a side street not far from the hotel where we stayed, one winter morning; a human resources manager pulled up and offered me a cashier assistant position at Costco. Unfortunately it was seasonal and after two months the assignment ended. The entire world believes I have a body odor issue. It's a lie from the pits of hell. When I was there, the store manager walked up to me and said, "Change your pad". I did not smell. He did not smell me. No customers smelled me either. If someone told him that, they were lying. I would never put myself in a professional setting or in an intimate situation, smelling; or thinking I may eventually smell and not care. There was no issue of that sort. But even if there were, it was unprofessional and inappropriate for him to say what he said, when he said it and where he said it. Think about it.

I had a serious boyfriend in middle school, (our families were very close). He is the current husband of my former high school girlfriend who went on the 9th grade trip to Europe with me. We never had sex and we obviously broke up. I refused to have sex in middle school; I wasn't ready nor married! But for some strange reason, a nationwide rumor is that I began having sex at age 9. I had a friend who was a boy, in Elementary school. His mother made my dress for my MISS TEEN Pageant and she was my cheerleading coach in Boys and Girls Club. They still live a few houses down from where I grew up. He used to swat me on my butt in the fourth grade. I even kissed him. I don't consider that real love or my first real kiss. (Even though I love him as a friend til this day). I didn't realize that he told everyone that we had sex. So sad. How rumors can try to dominate and destroy an innocent person's life.

In *Soul Food*, someone who does hair and gets back in touch with an ex-boyfriend; doesn't know how to cook. Now, the rumor is that I don't know how to cook. They'd heard about my ex-husband eating some chicken that wasn't all the way done and he ended up in the emergency room. (Well, neither I nor my daughter has gotten sick from my cooking within an 18 year period). They'd also heard that I'd gotten back in touch with my ex during high school. They believed that was why my marriage ended.

Another old rumor is, that my husband attacked me and tried to strangle me. He never punched me or choked me. (*Madea's Family Reunion*); the scenes of this movie are not true of my marital situation. The other rumor is that when I returned home after a failed marriage to my daughter's father, I was selling sex in my newly acquired apartment where my young daughter and I lived. I had a job which paid a salary that covered all of my expenses; (I'm a Christian. And even if I weren't, my breast aren't big enough to use my body that way, to earn a living, Lol). The marinating rumor is that I have sex with people I work with in order to be promoted. Another rumor is that I don't use bleach to wash my white clothes. The newest rumor is that I can't really talk, I just repeat what other people say.

Now this rumor, is huge. My medical information is given to others. Did someone put suicidal information in my charts after reading my poetry? It's just poetry. Everyone believe that I'm always having sex and always getting pregnant. This is supposedly why I smell. It's amazing that I didn't have reoccurring sexually transmitted diseases. My stomach has only looked pregnant when I had my daughter, before I broke-up with my then fiancée' and had my abortion, 15 years ago and when I was pregnant once and had a miscarriage during this homeless period. It's also amazing that it took leaving me friendless and homeless before I caught a disease that I cannot get rid of. I'm 40. Now my liver has to deal with processing medication on a regular basis. "Ok, now that she caught something, all the men believe she's talking to herself uncontrollably, and she's been conditioned like a pet dog, we can help her find a permanent place to live; just not with us."

I remember sitting at the laundromat one night and this guy walked up and talked to me for a while. He invited me to sleep in a spare room. His home was literally 3 houses down from the laundromat. I walked with him to the house. He had a pit bull and a lot of pet roaches. I quietly left, walked back to the laundromat and sat outside. (Do you see how this could cause a rumor)?

Ultimately I can't live down the fact that I made a mistake and had sex in the bathroom at work once with a guy who worked with a company adjacent to where I worked. Not random, but not appropriate....even though he and I went to lunch, hung out in his home, traveled by charter bus to Delaware to a casino, and went to a Tina Marie concert at Bull Run Park (all on different occasions of course); ultimately, he was already spoken for.

Now that this has happened, I suppose there are a lot of female pizza pies in my family. Yeah, O.K. mister pizza delivery guy; someone owes you $122.50. *Home Alone*. Each guy should give me $100 to get to know me because my jersey number is 22 and your goal is to make me sleep with 50 men. Unfortunately, I didn't get that message until the 20th time I watched the movie. (They thought I sold sex, they knew my jersey number and the plans for the movie, *Fifty (50) first Dates*, was already underway I suppose).

Hollywood, California felt that everyone should know about this mistake that I'd made. So they changed the facts, lied quite a bit and came up with an inappropriate, yet cute, cartoon called Shark Tale. It sabotaged my new teaching career for good. A career that was in full bloom ten years after this particular bathroom incident. I heard phrases one would never imagine coming forth from a second graders mouth. Ironically enough, two years after the movie had been made, way before I actually saw it, I'd lost my teaching job.

I had just lost my teaching job and wanted to unplug on the dance floor. I was offered a waitressing job by the manager soon after I arrived. (This nite-club had tables and served basic American foods). At the time I didn't realize the nite-club job had been sabotaged by the Shark Tale movie as well. I was being hated for no reason. I didn't smell. (I heard one patron ask another, "Do you smell her?") Why? Based on something they'd seen on TV.

Was I being profiled by the FBI or something? I accepted the position at the club because I needed a way to pay for my storage and I was now literally homeless. Sometimes I manned the coat closet. I doodled on my notebook and I danced with a co-worker to one of my favorite songs, but there was no telephone and oh yeah, we did not wash whales.

Had I known that I was being humiliated on shows that were geared for children, I would have chosen to go to graduate school for Journalism, not education? Now I have my grandson and I see why I was being harassed in class. He and I watch children's channels and shows all day.

I've always been a fan of Walt Disney. Disney Channel probably lost a lot of viewers for a short time. They finally removed the 'bring on the thunder' with the guitar in between his legs. That's really inappropriate to me. It seemed to remind me of the Run, Run Rudolph song that has my first love and first intimate partners name in the lyrics. (Just replace the "u" with an "a"). (Said Santa to a boy child, "What have you been longing for?" "All I want for Christmas is a Rock n Roll electric guitar"). Yes he and I exchanged presents. (I gave him a bible). I do not remember which flight it was but I was traveling alone and the flight attendant asked all of us who were catching the connecting flight to run to the other gate. I did not want to miss the flight even though her request seemed strange. Everyone ran. In the movie *Home Alone*, this particular song is playing in the background as the family runs to catch their flight during Christmas time.

Now my brother is a Descendant; the son of the Cruella de Vil on Disney Channel. The villain who wants to kill a large pack of 'dogs'; (puppies). I suppose they represent the men who've hurt me and my need for a coat as I stand in the cold as a homeless woman. (I haven't been intimate with half that amount of men; even though Hollywood and everyone else wanted the number to be 50). I will mention my brother when I send this letter off this week to the Supreme Court regarding my falsified ticket from DC and all of the black men who are being assaulted by the police. This to ensure his safety throughout this non-sense. He and I were raised right. We are not dumb or ghetto. He and I deserve justice for the violation of our rights. I've been married one time. My brother has been married three times but the women asked him.

One particular show on this channel, is mocking the taller thin red-head guy. At the beginning, they sing that they have each other's backs but they let him fall flat on his back. "You mean D-z said something profound?" says, another character. They are bullying his character and trying to crush me in real life. Ironically enough the only person whom I've known that shares his name, is a young woman who worked in the same company with me for a few years where I had a few failed relationships with men and made my 'big mistake' in the rest-room. I'd also shared with another co-worker that I'd kissed a woman before. The name they shared was very rare. She asked me if I was gonna 'come out'. I ignored her; I didn't really know what she meant but her tone seemed condescending. Now I guess she said it because she was gay. She'd never really talked to me before about anything other than work. We continued to work side-by-side in our office. I believe she was just helping out in our office for the day. She never made it a point to explain herself. But I didn't really care. No I am not crazy or paranoid.

Back to the reality of my homeless situation:

During this time, I was sleeping on the sofa of the clubs sound guy, for free. He was a really nice. No I did not sleep with him. But I did have one boyfriend while I was working there. He shared with me that his mom had passed away recently as well and he was having a tough time dealing with it. We went to a movie and we went bowling. We broke up right before I gave up the job at the club.

Not only did they, Hollywood and the FBI I presume, want everyone to know about my mistake; they wanted it to happen again. So EVERYONE cooperated and made sure that I had no place to live, no one to hug me, no friends, no cousins or anyone else to talk to or hang with and no income, for years. They then sent a knight in shining armor to 'swept me off of my feet' when I had absolutely nothing else to do and my brain was turning to mush. (In my heart and mind it was love and I was being spontaneous. It wasn't a one-nite, first date 'thing'). The men I was with when such incidents happened; (my only friend at that time), convinced (coerced) me into a position where we had sex in a place of business (when no one else was there) or at a park (when no one else was there). So the people who really were ho's, ended up getting there man. And I'm left to die; single. I guess that's why the artist said it sucks to be me. These were relationships with people I'd known well.

In the movie, the video director asked *Honey*, what she was doing and told her she was only working at the club for fun. I had briefly hung-out with a free-lance Film maker in California, with the same name as the video director in *Honey*. His mother was my mother's gynecologist. No he wasn't drunk; and no I didn't smack him. We did not kiss or touch at all; besides a friendly hug.

Back to reality on the east-coast:

If you happen to know about the main era in history when slaves were "slaves", then you may recall blacks were separated from their children, beaten, whipped; not allowed to read, or work for an income and forced to perform undesired sexual acts with people who weren't their mates. And you know, some slaves weren't allowed to think or speak the truth without consequence. (Now-a-days, slaves aren't even allowed to have any fun).

During this time when I was in my aunt's neighborhood, where my daughter and I stayed until I was forced to leave; I only had male visitors. No they did not stream in and out of her house but they were the only social contact I was allowed to have. You'll find that's a pattern in my life. It gives the wrong impression to a shallow mind looking from the outside, but a friend is a friend. I wasn't sleeping with these men, nor was I giving out blow jobs. I had a male teacher associate, from the school where I'd worked, who used to give me a ride to and from work. There was my male classroom assistant who was kind enough to run me to the grocery store when I needed to go. There was a man named Reggie that I ran into out and about and realized that we grew up in the same area. He stopped past one night and we sat in the car and talked. All we did was talk. {Why is there a woman (dressed as a Native American), making out in a car with a guy named Reggie, in *Welcome Home Roscoe Jenkins*; and someone standing outside of the car saying is that your cousin}?

There was a fellow teacher that I'd worked with at another school, who came and picked me up and ran me to get us dinner for the night; (for my daughter and I). He came in and watched a movie with my daughter and myself and then he went home. I was on my daily exercise walk through the neighborhood when I ran into an old Federal cop friend. He invited me to go to the neighborhood park so we could sit and talk. He talked about Sarah Palin as I sat on the picnic table listening. After he finished talking, I got up and he took my hand and pulled me toward him. I'd kissed him once before; before he told me he was married. I pulled back a little wondering if he was still married. Then glanced to my left and noticed I was in a scene from *The Princess Diaries 2* movie. Who and the hell are all of the people standing at the front of the park, starring at us? Forgive me for cursing Lord. I could have smacked him in his face. (I've never smacked anyone in the face). I didn't say that, but that's what I was thinking.

I also spent the night out with my boyfriend; who still wasn't treating me right. The one who I met at the carwash. The 7 year, on and off situation that just completely ended this year. (Could I be mentally slow? Was he the triple X being sent to me to make me fall?) Why couldn't females be sent to invite me out instead? I do not cheat in relationships and yes I like to have fun out-side of the house, as I get to know a man.

The relationships that I'd built as a child, with young boys and the ones I developed along the way; both came with sabotage already attached. God rebuilt my life after I'd made a few mistakes; only to be knocked down by those who didn't want me to succeed; which unfortunately is a massive number of people. Take away my chances of earning any kind of competitive income and stop me from having any fun. Discourage me from growing as I try to further my education. Verbally harass me anytime I actually get hired. Force me to sleep on an uncomfortable sofa in an apartment with bars on the window. Now act surprised that I absolutely believe you are all insane and being lead my satin himself. I'm grateful for this temporary shelter and I'm not complaining. This place would be great for 4 jail inmates, instead of a small bathroom sized living space; that is quite inhumane. (I'm not saying that because it's run-down. It's nice.)

I've heard it said that being incarcerated could possibly be better than being homeless. I guess the comparison is being done with regard to those who sleep on the ground, have no food and no means of income. Well here I am; Section D, Area K, Row 3, Site #8. If there's really a heaven, I guess death is better than homelessness too. No, I'm not in jail. But for me, death would probably be better than jail. No, I've never slept on the ground; but being in jail would definitely not be better than homelessness for me. I'm standing at my mother's grave. Ever since my mom passed away, I've been claustrophobic. I don't even ride elevators anymore. I wish I no longer had to break the laws of the land in order to pay for my storage unit, my basic health insurance and to buy my groceries. Yes, pan-handling is against the law. But it's my only form of income.

Although I didn't have a lot of disposable income. I did treat myself to a movie, to bowling a few times and to a few theatres plays that were only $6 during the day at the Publick Playhouse. (I already had my own ball and shoes).

When I left for college, I hadn't slept with anyone in my neighborhood. By the time I turned 30, there had been three people. And that's where the number stops. My husband was number six on my list of sex partners. If the people who knew me best don't truly know my heart and/or they refuse to make me a life-long partner, my chances anywhere else will be less. Now as hospitable as we were, we in turn were never invited to very many cook-outs other than by family members. Even if you don't want to marry me; why not invite me to your cook-out? Why not introduce me to your wife? Oh, you're pretending that you slept with me, because you want to. Now; (everyone); force me into situations where I have to get to know complete strangers and just be hopeful. Hopeful that they don't rape me. Hopeful that if he and I choose to start a relationship, we are both being honest and truthful. I'm not a liar or a ho. The song at the end of *Coach Carter* seems to have a certain ring to it.

Chapter 4

My Daughter and I - Deceived and Forgotten

You know it's funny, how a person sees things can transform how they view themselves and others; and ultimately, the world around them.

When I was forced to leave my daughter; it was her 7th grade year. Middle school in this state, is only two years. There's no school bus from or metro bus to get her there from the hotel where we stayed. It's a rural area. Seventh and eighth grade, she was there. I had been deceived by a couple of men and she thought I'd forgotten about her.

Supposedly; the reason why the entire world is against me is because I'm 'pretending' that men are deceiving me. Some folks believe I'm just dumb or I'm really a whore but I won't admit it.

Not only did my father say out of his mouth while standing in front of my open storage unit many years ago; you ain't never getting this stuff out of storage, but every relative I asked, refused to let me buy a shed and keep my belongings in their backyard. The crazy part about this statement is that everyone on the planet seemed to find joy in making my father's ludacris statement, come true. Hollywood just made

a movie to prepare me to sell my belongings. *Uptown Girls*. Photos that remind you of the great times you shared with family, never hung. Instruments that my daughter could have played, never used. Ten boxes of books. Brand new fancy kitchenware given to me as a wedding presents; never used. Thousands of business cards given to me while pan-handling, with a false sense of help attached; just stuck in the corner of a purse.

I must start with the point that the masses are trying to bring forth now. Implying that I had sex with strangers; implying that I let people sleep with me for shelter. The statement they're using is: "Oh you didn't know-you didn't have to sleep with them? The ones saying this, who truly believe what they're saying actually makes sense, must be the Anti-Christ. According to all the people in the world: from those in my neighborhood who've known me for 35 years, the millionaires living in Hollywood to the foreigners living in the bush; I'm the global ho. What they're saying is; I knew I was in a controlled environment in which all family members, former friends and neighbors left me homeless and I was I agreement with it (and I chose to have casual sex). (Think about it). Or they're saying, I wasn't in agreement with it; explaining my expressions of "drop some airplanes and shoot some folks"; because I really was doing it, but only because the entire world forced me to and I'm just mad about it because they're going to call me a ho forever because they chose this as my destiny. Everyone else, wants and has real love. But their crock of bull is just that. Simply sleeping outside/pan-handling and ruining my daughter's life, would definitely be enough to cause me to wish harm upon those who clearly were trying to kill us. Forgive me Lord.

"Trying to kill you; how?" Let me give o two great examples:

Well, I was standing on the median in Largo when a man drove up and offered to assist us with our situation. It was cold and I had caught the flu. He couldn't have come along at a better time. We had a hotel room but I was sick and so it was hard for me to get the money for the week. Why he came out to pick me up instead of his wife, I'll never know but they let me and my daughter sleep in their living room until I got over the flu. It was against their religion for a woman to be under the same roof with a married man. I left after finishing my prescribed medicine. I'd begun to feel better. They told her she could stay if she wanted. So she stayed, in case I wasn't able to get enough money for a room. Each day I got enough money for my hotel room and that was where I stayed. The school-year was coming to an end so we both thought it would be wise for her to stay where she was.

I was walking through another parking lot not far from where she was, pan-handling that next morning when a man and woman in an SUV gave me a business card. A few days later, I called him from the hotel that was nowhere near my daughter. He told me that he couldn't move one of his legs because of a permanent injury. Up until this moment, I'd turned down every man who asked if I could clean his house. He said he would pick me up and pay me for cooking and cleaning for him. I was then to return to an area where I could check into another hotel. When he picked me up, he told me the story of how he used to sell drugs and had been shot in the back and was now paralyzed from the waist down. He is wheel-chair bound and drives with his hands. We drove for 25 minutes on a two-lane road covered by trees. I was scared. I remembered the street names and could give someone directions to where I was located even though I had never been there before. It was a large house on a lot of land; in a neighborhood where, although you could see it, you had to drive to your neighbor's house. I cleaned and cooked and made a few phone calls from his home phone. I knew I didn't want to be there when it became dark. I rubbed his shoulders and we talked for a while. It was amazing that he lived way out there alone, and he was wheel-chair bound. We soon left. He drove me to a hotel where I checked in for the night.

It's amazing what's important to one person and not-so important to someone else. Talking and socializing is key to not losing brain cells. I have no phone. But when I had one, no one called except the one male friend I was allowed to have at that time. And he, no matter who he was; wouldn't treat me right; even if he considered himself my man.

No one on Facebook even talks to me. I guess coming to get their hair done would be out of the question. I would always see family at some point and they would complement me on my hair. Their hair would be broken and/or burned out from the root, but they would rather go bald or lose their edges, than give me $25 dollars to maintain their mane or put in the relaxer. The site says I have 576 friends, (and family). I didn't know what the issue was before, but now I'm the crazy homeless lady. Social media has made a mockery of every man, woman and child on the planet. Especially me. Nothings private. People added pictures of me to MY page without even asking. People added pictures of me from years ago; with other people, who could be serial killers by now!

I hurt most when I think about the friends and family who left. I didn't know until recently that they had seen allegedly incriminating movies about "me" and/or acquired information that led them to move very far away, (apparently from us). They left my daughter with me. Knowing that I wouldn't be able to work. They are proud of their children and their children are proud of themselves but these are people who when I was a child, used our spare room to rest when traveling and to live when homeless. People who broke bread with us at almost every cook-out we had, no matter how far they had to travel (probably 5 per year). I didn't realize that now, they all saw me as a worthless failure, whore.

My ex-husbands parents were pastors then and still are today. They live 1 hour from here, 10 minutes from her dad, who is now an ordained minister. How in the world did they explain leaving us homeless, to their church? And only God knows why a college educated, Christian man refuses to spend time with his own child. Breaks my heart.

There was my brothers' ex-wife who moved to Florida with their son; who was the same age as my daughter. She was remarried, for a while; to a man who resembled the dad in Cheaper By the Dozen. She took 10 foster kids and lived in a home with an indoor pool. She had a huge yard with a very tall fenced in area for their two large dogs. (I know she needed me as her personal assistant). The cousins who probably graduated cum laude and were now on the west coast, after moving there to practice law. (I know she needs me to do her hair). Former (life-long) friends who moved across the continent and were now working as surgeons and anesthesiologists. (I know she needs a before and after care provider and her sister needs me as her maid). A former school-mate who moved down south and worked in a doctor's office in Fort Lauderdale- and/or former friend and co- worker who was a Pharmacist right here in our town. None the less, they left my daughter here, to suffer with me! (Not to mention all of the former neighbors, known long enough to be family, who could have taken us in. They know half the stuff on TV and in the movies is about them anyway).

I wasn't thinking about saving the world at age 15, so I wanted to write commercials for a living. Little did I know that I would need the rest of the world to "save" me; one dollar at a time (*"Madea's Witness Protection"*). Well, they have all made it seem as though I'm the slacker who needs saving. (No I do not rob people). Although I've made mistakes, I'm glad Jesus saved me long ago. I stood on the median with the homeless sign until the police gave me so many citations that I no longer had that as a means of income. I then began walking from parking lot to parking lot humbly; all day, every day; asking for spare change (I was never dirty or torn-but sometimes I did smell like outside). For three odd years, I did this to keep her in a hotel rather than a shelter or in the home of some lunatic. Our hotel had a kitchen so I was able to cook for her. She finally graduated and is now in college, working two jobs and she was able to save enough with me, to purchase herself a nice used car.

I'll never really understand why my father chose to move so far away and not invite us with him but when my mother passed away, he left and my daughter's life was run- a-muck after I lost my job. He dropped the ball when we needed him. He didn't come back to get us. Unfortunately he's found a peace in an old hobby; baking. But he lives alone, and well... eating an entire pie or cake isn't very healthy. He ended up having to get a pace maker in his heart. Although *BAPS* wants you to think so. I'm not waiting for him to die. I can't believe that no one from either of the churches that he has been so loyal to, offered to drive me and my daughter down to him. Remember we didn't have a car and I'm unable to ride charter buses. Trust me once before I tried to catch a charter bus down to my dad I NC because I could hear the bronchitis in his chest. I made it from New Carrollton to DC. It was challenging. I ended up snowed in and sleeping at the DC bus station. Everyone else was stuck there too. A kind employee at the station was headed to NC as well. He gave me a ride to my dad's.

My only sibling was living in Miami with his girlfriend. Unfortunately, he is still unemployed as well, I believe. He's been down there ever since he got out of the Marine Corp. He's a great guy. In fact I believe part of the reason why I was so naive when it came to relationships with men, is because the men in my own family, were great. My grandfather, father, brother and my uncles were kind to women. Coming out of my marriage, I had no idea so many black men were such pathetic womanizers. I guess my girlfriends and cousins didn't have their dad around or were hurt my males in high school and college. Who knew?....... Ask them and they'll tell you they're just smarter than me. Or they'll probably say I was insecure and being a ho.

Everybody's Helping

Now, the most paralyzing part of this situation is that, the word *help* has taken on an entirely new definition to the human world. When I ask for 'help' in a specific area; like needing shelter for my daughter and myself, that's ignored. When I ask for hair clients; they shy away. (But they can come out of their home, talk briefly for 1 minute as I pan-handle; give me $5, then leave me standing there; after we've prayed that my situation changes).

(It's a little bazaar to sabotage someone and then go out of your way to make it seem like they need you to get their life back on track. They're helping me because they're smarter and kinder. If you say so).

Everybody what's to take credit for the ideas in this book. I didn't ask for help in that area nor do I believe I need it. Why couldn't they just help when I asked for permanent shelter for me and my daughter?

The year is 2015 and already I'm getting more 'hateration' than one homeless woman can stand. "You're wearing a Columbia jacket", one strange woman says as she passes me by as I stand pan-handling at 7-eleven 7:30 am to catch the morning rush. And "You're awfully fly to be homeless", one strange man says as I walk and (pan-handle) in the parking lot of the local Giant grocery store, as he attempts to get my number and offer me a ride. I took his number and bid him farewell. Gee, it was on clearance and I put it on lay-away at Burlington, I said out loud to myself. I have accepted that this planet has made me the 'designated homeless' destined to be single and friendless. (Now they don't even want me to be warm). I thank God that I did receive the amount of money I needed to get the groceries and items I needed before the storm arrived. It took a lot longer than usual.

I hadn't given up on trying to earn a living using my talents. I walked by faith in another attempt to jump start my cosmetology career.

I stopped pan-handling, went to a church run shelter program called warm nights for 2-3 months while I sat in a salon and called back all the folks who had given me business cards. Even during this adventure; I was being set-up for failure. Keep in mind that I can only ride in the 15 passenger shelter van, is if I ride in the front seat; it's too closed in. I was forced to ride in the vehicle of the old, disabled, white, male veteran who stayed there too, but provided his own transportation. (It gave the appearance of a young black prostitute riding around town with my pimp or daily client; but I was grateful to him non-the-less). (My daughter was still with my family at first). So that my daughter could be with me after the shelter program ended, I rented a room with a hair client the other odd months while still working at the salon. The unknown clients that God sent to me, eventually supported me enough so that I was able to pay $150 per week for our room and $150 per month for my storage. I did this for an entire year. Unfortunately, that wasn't enough to pay for other expenses and responsibilities that I struggled to pay that year by doing hair and pan-handling in between. Well, now I guess they'll be no more citations from the cops. I ended up pan-handling full-time. She and I briefly returned to the hotel because my clients daughter moved back home with her new baby.

I must share with you what happened while I was staying in one of the churches. The program was set up where we slept in a temporary rooming area inside of a new church in the region, every week. We were in the auditorium of one church preparing to have dinner when I glanced at the evening News on the large screen television. My mouth fell and I was almost speechless. Oh my God was all I could get out of my mouth. The female broadcaster on Channel 2 a young woman who had grown up in a near-by neighborhood, participated in the same Boys and Girls Club as I, and graduated from the same college as I had. I was happy for her but that is the first TV station that I took my resume to upon graduating. I didn't have any experience. Well anyway, I wonder if she likes the show Being Mary Jane. What difference does it make, I'm sure she's married with children.

It's a shame that we couldn't live with my aunt who housed my 94 year old grandma before she passed away. That particular aunt worked more than one job. You would think that she, myself and my daughter would have been able to all live with my dad at his new home in N.C.. She was home during the day by herself. Everyone acted as if I was the only one on earth who could go over and talk to her. (Maybe she was being held against her will like me).

Mind you, I was standing outside on the median in freezing cold temperatures just to keep a roof over me and my daughter's head. Now I believe they wanted me to be the red headed girl just breaking into the writing industry from the movie, The help. In this particular movie the actor/actress says,"Everybody knows I'm not going to get a man in this town so I might as well leave quickly." I suppose this is because I've been the homeless lady for so many years. I don't want to be a robot or a puppet. (I'm not doing what they say, they are predicting). I loved my grandmother. She lives on in my heart. I didn't spend the one on one time with her that you would think. She lived with an aunt who had recently assaulted me. (Thirty-five years and now my family had gone crazy). I can only pray that I can walk without a cane at age 94. The secret must be staying free of men; forever.

This paragraph should probably be at the end of my book because it just happened; however, it is a perfect example of what I mean when I say everyone has changed the definition of the word help. My father was in town last week. He and my daughter talk quite often, from what I understand. But after he paid for my daughter's car, in full; the brand new one that she qualified for on her own; and we'd all gone to dinner for my birthday, he took me to the grocery store and I filled the cart. He was helping me pick my groceries. I do not need anyone to help me pick my groceries. It just hurts so much to think about what I really need and the fact that I can't get him to understand. I need a bed to sleep in. I needed a car a long time ago. I need a place to live where I don't have to pay right now, and so does she. We are family and we should be together. Including my brother. My father is smart. He knows it's important that a person learn how to do certain things for themselves or they may never appreciate things the way they should. It's probably best that she qualified on her own first. However, we are both literally killing ourselves to just to keep a roof over our heads. She's working two jobs. I'm pan-handling to have basic health insurance. There are so many reasons why we should not be living in this particular apartment. Sudden death has so many ways that it could overtake us. I thank God for His protection and the blood of Jesus that covers us but we also need to be wise.

I may not be the wisest one in the bunch but you would never hear me say to a homeless woman; "The men are only offering you a place to stay so that you will sleep with them; so start with your legs closed." The previous statement leads me to believe that I'm definitely not the dumbest.

We were now renting a room in a home, with random strangers. I pay for the room by pan-handling and my poor baby girl has to catch the metro bus to school. This is one of the homes where I was physically assaulted by a drunken woman who was renting a room there as well. We ended up back at the hotel. It was more expensive but a better solution in the long run.

Chapter 5

Venting About My Demise

Anytime you do anything that causes anyone to be less productive in society, it's not smart. It wasn't during homelessness but I must share this story. This was before the new millennium. Not only had my former girlfriend from my younger days, (that I had on I just recently bumped into), stood me up for our planned outing to a Howard Univ. fight party. But when I got there, alone; not one woman spoke to me. There were a lot of people there. I could have networked for employment. Communications, Media, Hair; something. They ignored me. Waiting for the fight to come on, a naked stripper laid at my feet. I immediately got up and went into the room with the TV. I watched some of the fight then I walked back into the living room. A guy in the fight room who had spoken to me briefly, invited me up to the next level in the home. Oh no honey, I'm not here for that, I thought to myself. I said good-bye. (Nothing happened). By the time I got to the bottom of the stairs, there was another guy who struck up a conversation with me. He could see the absolute horror in my face. How could they be so mean? We walked outside and he invited me to his apartment. He lived at the top of the building. The view was outstanding. I took in the view as we talked and hung out for quite some time. I guess I left home to watch the fight, make some friends and to find someone to talk to. Now I have him to talk to. But it's really late and I'm a long way from home. I chose to stay. And we had sex. The next morning, he drove me back to my car. No my car had not been ticketed where I was parked. (Never did hear back from my girlfriend until a few months ago as I pan-handled in the parking lot. It's been many years). She gave me her number. I threw it away). A few days later, I showed up unannounced at his door. He was flabbergasted. Why haven't you been answering the phone? My first and only one-nite-stand, ever. These were black people.

Did you know that if you are able to hear and speak and no one talks to you for extremely long periods of time; that is painful and abusive? (And yes, you lose brain cells). So when you ask if I'm hurt with the assumption that it's because I'm single, you are incorrect. Even though she should not have said that in that particular movie because she had plenty of people to talk to, the writer knew what I was dealing with. And if the writer knew; I'd have to imagine, God knew. *Jumping the Broom*. But that does not give you the right to harass me in any way. Nor should you spend thousands of dollars to make a movie mocking me by saying 'Lord forgive me for having sex for a little conversation' (*Jumping The Broom*) even if you and everyone else know that he is the ONLY person on the planet allowed to talk to me; literally! (Oh, that's supposed to be me? Look how she's dressed, in *Hitch*. Because I worked in a club? We wore a uniform.) And I don't rob Peter to pay Paul; *Just Wright*. Now I have brain damage from standing in the cold and from not having stimulating conversation; in real life! (It's the United Cult of America)! Oh wait, I get it, she's not trying to say I dress like that; she's saying that guys would rather have a waitress that looks like her. The nutty part is that my parents are both my birth parents. Now, I do have a cousin who may not have found out until she was in elementary school, that her dad was not her birth father. And I guess it's just a coincidence that when my entire extended family went to that particular cousins home for an overnight, family birthday party, I invited my (former) life-long girlfriend who happens to have the same name as the **tag along guest** in the movie. We all love my cousin dearly. We call her the nick-name her mom gave her. She's the **most famous of all the fairies**. I also have a former girlfriend who drives the same car that the bride in the movie was driving when she almost ran-over her husband. (She was in that same car when she rode past and gave me $20 as I stood on the median with my homeless sign years ago). And supposedly, **my former nurse**

friend never had sex with him until she was married. I wonder if **the three of them** are being harassed verbally. Just like I'm about to break this down for you to change the way you see the facts. The same could be done for me by someone else. But that will never happen.

Now if you drop the 'R' in the name of the tag-a-along guest; you come up with a similar name. It's pronounced the same but spelled with an 'S' and she is a manager that used to work with me on the job where I made out with a man who worked in an entirely different region but within the same company. (After the guy with the floor buffer left- *The Day After Tomorrow*). He was not my boss. Her child went to the same elementary school that my daughter attended. She was my boss at one time. I know she would tell you I was a hard worker and that I did more than what was expected of me. I assume she saw me before I saw her; one day at the school. She slowly walked up to me and said with a sinister look, I've seen enough or we've seen enough. I just said hello excitedly and spoke to her briefly. I'm not ashamed of anything I've done. I didn't do it to get promoted. She must have advanced to the next level of management since I'd left and was in the room when the tape was shown of me and him in the office in Sligo Creek. Or she's speaking to someone who's not there, telling them that they've seen enough of 'my' personal information on TV and in movies. Yeah I liked him and all I could think was love. If you infer 'ho' from that; that's on you.

I'm sure your paradigm would shift if I tell you that each of these three women called me after reading my book, sharing with me their similar stories of having sex 'too soon' with a man. (Maybe one of them actually prayed after sex and said exactly what she said. Maybe one of them slept with a man who looked just like that guy). Or maybe if I share with you that a guy with the exact same first and last name, that looks exactly like the guy she marries in Jumping The Broom was dating a girl who looked a lot like the girl in the movie; at the college where I received my Bachelor's degree.

I can't believe this many human beings are this dumb and/or mean.

College educated people of every race. You really think it's 'help' that I need; not normal-minded kind people (as in friends and family). Any normal-minded adult that needs help, can seek help by asking for it. But if God has NO ONE to use, then that person will not be a part of living society. I'm not really 'missing it' in many areas of my life as much as I am having 'it' withheld from me or taken from me intentionally. I can't tell you what 'it' is; either you get it or you don't. Either you are nice or you aren't.

Although I truly have no adults to talk to, I enjoy talking to my one year old grandson. I will just continue talking to him, until he can talk back. He's my heart. I haven't had sex since he's been born and do not intend to.

I'm not an actress. I don't live in Hollywood. Why is EVERYBODY so obsessed with everything that I do? The answer is clear. They can focus the attention on me and then they don't feel so bad. Pathetic millionaires. Then they can say, the ho is that girl on the East-Coast, not us. (Only problem with saying the girl on the east-coast now, is that the one with the 'two bee stings' who used to drive a Rav-4 before she became rich, now lives on the West-Coast; and she's not a ho either). If they keep me poor, they can make it seem like I'm pressed. This is not 300 pages of paranoia. Can I just earn some money so that I can enjoy myself; help my brother if he needs me; pay some over-due bills, (so I won't go to jail) and take care of my daughter and grandson? Not to mention, I would love to use the talents that God has given me. Life is short. I don't believe my father needs my help but if he does, of course I want to help him as well. And when it's all said and done, God can use me much more if I have a little money.

Back to the subject at hand; pan-handling:

I must give this example in hopes that you will understand my heart. I stood at the entrance to a neighborhood in Largo for an entire winter, for $122 per day. I got just enough money each day. I couldn't go to church! I stood on the median in the freezing cold. A kind man, with a nice car, who owned a very nice home in this affluent neighborhood, invited me to have Thanksgiving with him and his daughter. (I believe he was ex-military). My daughter and my soon to be son-in-law were at the hotel. They both had places to go for Thanksgiving. I chose to spend Thanksgiving alone in my hotel room. He said he needed someone to fix his meal. He had all of the food already in this kitchen. He was nice looking and he had a nice home. I'm not looking for a man, 'I thought to myself'. (His daughter was college age). I cooked and then I left. (For some reason, now I can have a decent man as my friend! No thanks! I am not a ho! The entire planet forced me to befriend this terrible man for five years! (I believed he loved me). The man that I had been seeing for 5 years, I loved him; but he was not a good person for me. The only reason I even let him in, the last time I saw him, was because I didn't believe he had anywhere to stay and I was trying to prove to him that he couldn't share a room with me because he can't keep his hands to himself. And he couldn't. No I did not have sex with him.

This is you, speaking to me. "But you knew someone was watching you. Just do the right thing." Oh. Do the thing that you believe is right so that you can make a movie about what you believe would have been the right decision, but then botch the story with other lies? I don't have a job and you've just about ruined my daughter's life. What does your perspective on my life have to do with the price of tea in China? All of the families and strangers she and I were forced to live with. What if someone cut their finger while cooking; HIV; hepatitis, etc....(People we trusted, who served us food in their homes).

What kind of person basks in knowing that they played an intricate part in creating a real-life nightmare for a, hard-working, single-parent. These writers and producers have taken my life's mohill of mistakes and turned them into a mountain of disaster; making sure that they cause others to believe I am not worthy of a healthy, fun, monogamous relationship with the opposite sex or a culturally enriching relationship with an educated friend of the same sex. And the people in my community or my former social circle have crucified me; and it's unjustified. There are a lot of murderers, rapists, thieves, drug-dealers and gold diggers on the street. They all have friends and most have a significant other. Some are even able to write a book and earn an honest living from it. (One needs to have a social circle of supporters, to sell a book). These people's offenses seem to be forgiven and forgotten. If we never let go of others mistakes and always harshly judge what they do, how can God heal us when we pray or forgive us when we ask. And no I'm not saying I was being a ho, because I wasn't.

The disheartening part is that I'm a Christian. No I do not belong to a church anymore. I have been saved since I was very young. My own grandfather was a pastor. I truly love the Lord, but I have no desire to worship in a sanctuary for fear of harassment. I rarely have time to get to church because I babysit my grandson (for free) and I'm pan-handling all the other time. (My daughter doesn't want him on the bus.) But ultimately, how do you worship with people who don't care if you're homeless? Even people on the street who never mentioned Jesus, took me in out of the elements. And they didn't ask for sex- Nor did I offer it.

When I first became homeless; standing on the median; an older white guy offered me an opportunity for my daughter and myself, to move with him to a county an hour away from where we currently were. Were they actually trying to force me to be in a relationship with an old white-man, to live out another upcoming TV situation; (*Modern Family*) maybe. Was his estranged wife's name, Sofia the First? Or was this my penis with the lottery ticket on it? *Deliver Us From Eva*. (OK maybe he just looked older than he was.) He got mad after I refused. He shouted, what better offers do you have!...... Unbelievable, I said to myself. Oh yeah, during this time, I also turned down a few men who drove past and asked if I would suck their penis' for well over $100. The answer was "no".

My daughter and I lived with 5 different families where there was a married couple involved. No I did not sleep with any of their husbands. (These weren't strangers.)

God made it so that I was able to pan-handle and pay for a hotel with a kitchen. My daughter never had to stay in a shelter. For three years, I paid per day /per week to live independently with my child. Ninth grade; renting rooms with strangers was brutal. The way other people live is interesting. Violence and alcohol...Well; God found us our own hotel room with a kitchen, for half the price. It was built while we were homeless.

Now during these five years, I had my very own man. (The other relationship that ended this year).

If I choose to have my man over to have sex with me during his lunch time, then that is my business. I repent before God but I don't owe anyone an explanation. Especially the people who forced me into homelessness. (I lived with this man's sister for a month when we first met; again, before my daughter was with me.) He eventually moved there too. He said he was staying at his cousins. Now, if you happen to know that he is cheating on me, (and you refuse to talk or socialize with me); and I don't know he's cheating, your paradigm is different.

There was one particular year toward the end of my intentional isolation; (homelessness); where it was obvious that everyone was determined to force me to have sex with a random stranger. Not placing blame; just stating facts. (Yes it was during a time when my man was obviously having a brain fart). Actually, (he was a part of the cult too.) I couldn't reach him for several weeks. As far as I was concerned, we were done; and no I wasn't looking for him because I was horny. Now think. If I wanted to sell sex, I could go into the neighborhood where I grew up and organize a list of sex clients. I worked in a club. It would have been easy to put together a list of sexual clients. If I was pressed to have a penis in my vagina or desperate for a man to marry me, why wouldn't I just go to a singles events at church; hang at a bar; frequent a club; or join Match.com. Or just walk up to someone on the street and say let's have sex; *I think I love my wife.* (I watched this movie once and the actor/(actress) laid on the bed and said, you may smell something.) Well, I guess everyone mistakenly believes I said that.

Trust me when I stayed on base at Andrews and my daughter went to her friend's house, the guy put me up in a 'bad' villa; in the middle of the woods. It was nice. (The Presidential Inn was full of returning soldiers). A big picture of Ulysses S. Grant hung on the wall. I sat reading about him, waiting for the president to come in and say he wants to be with me! He never showed up. So I don't know who the *Scandal* character is.

I was literally able to prove to myself that I have no true friends nor do I have any family members who are truly walking in the love of God. I also proved that someone is watching me and wants me to be in a situation where I'm so hurt that I hug anyone who wants to hug me. They want me to fall sexually to create a whore image; don't want to be my friend; but don't want me to catch a disease. I was not ho-ing, as you folks say. (**My race. Something is wrong with yawl!**) I was renting a room in a home and my daughter was on the telephone. (There were no other options for me to rent. Days Inn made me leave because the girl in the room next to me was a prostitute but the people were parking in front of my room. The police knocked on my door and everything- I was alone).

I sat in the living room to give my daughter privacy and to get away from the annoying non-stop conversation between her and her boyfriend. A man was renting a room in the same house as the two of us and a woman upstairs, renting as well. Yeah, we went to a museum and to a movie. He and I had been conversing for some time but I eventually went in his room so that I could continue to have someone to talk to who wasn't on the phone constantly; (my daughter). He looked like he may have a disease. He was very thin. His skin was clear but he was extremely thin. When it seemed as though he and I were getting closer, the woman from upstairs yells, "No she doesn't have that!" We hadn't and we weren't having sex at the time. I did it on purpose. Yawl are mean as hell and dumb as all get out! You have no idea how hurt... not because I didn't have a man. Then you have the audacity to verbally harass me! (This was not the socialization I desired.) He takes medicine for his mind. No I did not continue the relationship. (I guess I caught him on a day when he hadn't taken his medicine). (A mixed descendant of a former U.S. president).

If I'm all about the penis and making my vagina cum; why did I call my former next door neighbors in North Carolina to ask if I could live with them; from day one? I guess your attempt to make it seem as though I'm running men in and out of my dwelling and your plan to force me to have random strangers as friends; wouldn't have worked, had I been able to move down south with them or my father. They lived next door to us for 25 to 30 years. It's like now she's Sofia the First, when Sofia grows up and gets her own place. I guess I thought I could at least be Baileywick for her aging parents. Well what's her name, you wonder? Can't tell you her name but her nick-name is the Spice living on Gilligan's Island. My father lives alone, one county over from them. He locks his doors from the inside and takes out the key. I can't breathe unless I sleep with the key in my hand. It's scary. My father has always been able to talk; he just never listened. And that is still a struggle for him. He just cuts you off, and makes is point. But now that he is saved, he's much kinder. He has always meant well.

I couldn't pan-handle (police), I had no job (bad credit), no friends (I'm a ho), no family (I'm lazy), no place to sleep (I must be a hooker) and I looked just fine (I must be stealing), I smelled fine (I must stink) and I was in my right mine (I must be crazy). I read the local newspaper while riding on the bus. I stretch and do sit-ups every morning (I must be angry). And my hair is long and healthy (must be a wig). The entire planet earth is making sure that I do not have to steady income above the bare necessities, (Their mean and pressed). My teeth are all accounted for, straight and white-ish-{tea stains from trying to stay warm. I visit the dentist on a regular basis. ("Don't talk, just smile; you're slow")}. No one actually said this but it was pretty much what everyone in my life whom I had ever had a relationship with (man, woman or child), was saying; without saying a word.

Here's another major wave of sabotage. I sat in the salon; they refused to come get their hair done. We were all forced to leave the Warm Nights Christian Run, Shelter Program way before it was scheduled to end. The public metro bus never showed up to take me to work in the freezing cold. (All of these things could not have been a coincidence). I ended up accepting a ride to work from a strange man who asked for my telephone number. Later that day, with empty pockets, he picked me up from work and I went with him to his home where his mother and sister sat. She didn't offer me a room. He got all of his belongings. Now I know that the argument he was having with his mother, must have been staged. But when I was there, had I thought they were joking, I would have asked her if I could stay in her home. I'd had zero clients this particular day. I went with him to a hotel. (At that very moment; that was where we both lived). When I arrived I took a shower alone, got fully dressed in the bathroom, put on fitted jeans with a belt and a turtle-neck. I spent one night there and realized that I needed to try to pan-handle again so that I could get my own room; even if the police approach me like before. It was not my desire to sleep with any man but especially not to a man I barely know. And no, it wasn't casual. And I wasn't 'ho-ing'. I think you all are confused. It is at these moments that I feel larger than life. The women who forced me into such a situation, are the women that the men want to be married to. Why would I think that this is a controlled environment and I just need to say no and then everything will be OK? This situation makes me realize everyone is sicker than I think. You're just a bunch of sickos! Any tears that come after a moment like that aren't because I've been destroyed emotionally. Isn't it obvious? Once this happened a few times, then I don't have to be homeless anymore. Here I am. Sleeping on my daughter's sofa.

This is you;" Whatever; she is not hurt, she just a ho!" And to that, I say. "You're uneducated and ghetto". And to those saying,"Aww; Because she's hurt." "You're dumb, and mean." But what about those who say, "Of course; she's homeless." "You're insane and mean." I'm not a ho nor a liar. And I don't have casual sex. I'm not pressed for a man. It's like you all have amnesia. Read this book one more time. Pay very close attention. I know how to say no and I'm not horny.

Either this non-sense of 'sleeping here and then there,' is being orchestrated by my family and friends or they are very lucky. Trust me, if I had caught HIV during this homeless situation, we would all be in heaven having a talk show about why they left me outside. My daughter has an apartment now. Trust me, this country does not want me to move out of here and back into a hotel, pan-handling, full-time, again. Oh, I will, but you don't want that. Trust me. But something has to give. She's so busy that I barely get to go outside and pan-handle. She can't afford to feed me. I'm in need of comprehensive health coverage ASAP. I had coverage but my daughter had a baby so she has her own plan now and the State said I no longer qualified. (Either way, she would have been a way at college and/or over 18, so carrying her would no longer be an option. I don't get any benefits from the State.

You are all blithering idiots and you're mean as hell. Think about it! How can I go to church and worship with people who would force a single mother into such situations. I don't care that no man wants me. I went to church first! I wrote letters; I made phone calls; oh my God! I'm now being harassed by the people on the bus. I'm not a whore. And I'm not crazy. I'm closed now, they say. Yuck. I have no desire what so ever to be married or to be friends with women who wanted me to fall. It was bad enough that the relationships with my (former) life-long, male friends, didn't work-out. Apparently, I was set-up in the situation with this guy, by (friends) enemies, for him to see if I smell. The church wanted to see if I would fight him off and say no. I hadn't told anyone. But people seemed to already know. You all are pathetic.

Maybe, had they made sure their children were prepared and orderly in class, they wouldn't have had so much time to focus and obsess over me and my daughter? The haters can say that I'm making excuses all they want. Even deaf people who can't speak, need to communicate. I have to talk to someone. I have to socialize with someone. Even people with no arms, need to be touched. (Hugged). I'm not a horny airhead. I don't make a habit of being intimate on the first date nor did I sleep with everyone I've dated. You all need Jesus. And what black man in his right mind wants to use any black woman for sex. As black people, we have enough non-sense to deal with as it is.

I've supervised many classrooms on every grade level, as a substitute teacher (while attempting to pass the Praxis Exam as I attempted to change my career field to Education); so I really shouldn't be surprised at how many morons there are in our society; black people are just idiots. I can't stand being around them. Especially the ignorant, loud, uneducated ones on the bus, in the grocery store, in the library and at church. We go out of our way to try to kill each other; physically and emotionally. Maybe white people are just as dumb, but given their history with us, you kind of expect the strange thinking and off-the-wall rationale, to give way to harassment and intentional sabotage.

God knows the truth and he knows the reason that you have me walking around outside for income! The purpose of this book is not so that you can count the people you believe I slept with. My civil rights are being violated. There's nothing wrong with me. I'm not loose or crazy. There's something wrong with you all. Why would sane, Christian family members and friends say, we're enjoying our lives and you're not?

Are you still wondering, where are all of the Christian women when a Christian sister needs help? Oh, they're not helping me because they don't believe I'm a Christian, I see. This is the way I want things to be.

With an entire world against me; You are more than enough- Lord God. As long as God knows I'm not a ho or a liar, at this point, that's all that matters.

The female Union

My Christian sorors will probably spend an entire day witnessing and doing out-reach with their church; but they won't be my friend. There's no Christian soror to take me and my daughter in?

So 6 years after I've been homeless and none of them have invited us to stay, they finally have a get-together. In a public restaurant. Only 3 sorors show up. They sit there and stare at me as if they are waiting for me to start mumbling at the mouth. They act as if it's strange that I seem to be speaking louder than I should, indoors. But then, as we leave, they tell me they love me. I just don't understand. I don't have to live with you for you to be my friend. I'm not pressed for a man. You are all just trying to force me to only have male friends.

Now these three sorors: 1st; her last name in real-life is the first name of the husband of the irate female character in "Why Did I Get Married"; the one who wrote the book and smashed the items in the living room; (She married right out of college too); 2nd, her real-life first name is the same as the lead singing character in the movie, Hairspray; she's cute but kind of chunky. And 3rd; You know the actual first name of the groom in the Best Man; that's her last name in real-life.

If and when I begin to have female friends again, it will be because their behavior changes, not mine. I'll pray that God changes their hearts and they apologize.

I'd managed to get through 16 years of schooling without intentionally dating, or befriending a man or woman who had been in jail, done drugs, or smoked (around me). (It's a completely different situation when you've been friends for 30 years prior and that person is charged with breaking some kind of law much later in life). You may choose not marry him or her because of the mistakes but the friendship is already there. And no, I'm not a talking about myself. They at least deserve a conversation with you if you happen to run into him or her. Listen to his or he side. I am not a criminal. I don't smoke, I don't even sip alcohol anymore. And when I did, it was never in large consumption and never around strange men, except for one or two exceptions when I may have accepted a glass of wine against my better judgement.

Now keep in mind that as I explain everything, over an approximate 15 year period, there will not have been one invitation by a woman, to me; formal or informal, to go anywhere. No regular talks on the phone or regular socializing of any sort. I thank God that I'm NOT mumbling uncontrollably to myself. My daughter is just about 19. For the first 4 years or so when I returned to the area, people associated with me; and I had friends...... that soon ended.

I clearly remember what went on in my life during that time period. It wasn't prostitution or wild behavior. I was focused and a lot of people were interested in me. I wasn't aware of every movie or TV show that was being created that was sabotaging my character, or what it may have looked like to my neighbors who may have noticed only male company entering my apartment. I do know that whatever the women were watching as entertainment, must have lead them to want to stay away from me. And whatever the men were watching, must have lead them to believe that they needed to get to know me. I didn't realize that something strange was happening until I had lost all of my friends; male and female. (The strange thing that was happening wasn't me being a ho, it was me being sabotaged from every angle; I'm not talking about sex). I didn't find it strange that people were gravitating to me because I believed I was beautiful, kind and worth getting to know. (Now I realize the days that I ran into old friends, male and female, was probably not by chance). My relationships with men, were appropriate; so were the friendships I had with women. But now, for some reason, all of my (real) life-long friendships are gone. I can be your friend and not live with you. They're cute, they have titty's, they have money but they've all grown up to be unfriendly, (working) *Desperate Housewives*. Did all of these former male friends after talking to me once, say they slept with me?

Now, if you have no friends or family who socialize with you regularly and you're forced to be friends with people who are not of like character for an indefinite amount of time, (before and during the time you were left homeless); find love with a few of those select people at different times (not sex, love); and the relationship doesn't work-out, why would you be thoroughly harassed around town, about your private relationships? Unless, the plan all along was to ruin your reputation.

The plan wasn't to set me free (outside) with the hopes that I find love, but to simply put me in a situation where calling me a fowl name seems appropriate.

It's really sad that because everyone believes that I don't know how to do hair; that I smell and that I'm a ho and may have a contagious disease that may radiate from my hands through their scalp, I'm unable to earn a living using my cosmetology license. I see how black people may have become slaves. Look how they treat their own people. The way I smell is not an issue; period. My pad is changed when it needs to be and/or on a regular basis depending on the situation. I stay in tune with my body. My vagina is not smelly. I do not wear clothing twice to work before washing them.

I was the Student Government President in the 8th grade. Yes I was an honor student throughout my years of schooling. I worked hard at projects and excelled in academics and extracurricular activities for many years. I was co-editor of the yearbook my Junior and Senior year.(Not sure how my name got left out of the Class Officers picture Senior year). I took challenging Advanced Placement courses. (I had a 3.0 or higher every semester since Kindergarten except the one where I took Astro-Physics; *Armageddon*.) (I excelled at Physics and Geometry in high-school. Both of those teachers were awesome. They made it fun.) I finished college with a Bachelor's Degree in Mass Communications within 4 years. I acquired a trade license one year after that and worked in that field for quite some time while my daughter was young and I could make my own hours. After some life altering let-downs. I took several graduate level courses in order to prepare me to change fields to education as I worked as a substitute teacher. I certainly could have become a doctor or an attorney many years ago. I haven't achieved like my girlfriends had expected. I continued to thrive and maintain a happy, peaceful, fun life for me and my daughter; up until the day I lost my job in the school system and was left homeless.

But no matter whether I'd known these women from the neighborhood where I'd lived since age two, whether I met her at age 9 on the community basketball team, or whether I met her at church; they never kept in touch..............Oh wait I would usually go to clubs and dance by myself (after my divorce, in my mid-twenties). Once I did go to a nite-club with my high-school friends from the track team. I danced all night. That's not weird. But they still didn't keep in touch. And yes, my Christian, soror did help me move my stuff from one storage unit to another 7 years ago. ('Ok *Daddy Daycare*; (singing) "Momma's alright, daddy's alright I just seem a little weird.")

I confess with my mouth- that socially, life will get better. I cherish the day. Don't get me wrong I used to stay quite busy with my large extended family. Nearly 75% of family gatherings were held at our house. . . My dad was a cheapskate but he surely didn't mind buying food. We always invited everybody. Me and my dad were two of the friendliest, most hospitable, people you would ever want to meet, but now that I look back and currently sit here friendless, I guess nobody liked us. Well..... I guess someone liked us both at some point though. We've both been married.

I have attended all of my high-school class reunions. They were nice. I was, or I guess you can say I still am, the class president. I planned the first reunion. It was great to see everyone. I was really surprised at all of the people who did not come. (Yes, for 4 years I was the president of my graduating class in high school). A young woman whose name is on my face in The Best Man and the Princess Diaries Movies, has taken the reigns. She's rich (because she's smart and talented), and I'm poor. The father, of her child; who shares my daughter's middle name, is a famous basketball player. 'What's his name!" Just calm down. I'll give you a hint: (Did the people at Howard University see Juwanna Mann?)

I bet you didn't know there was another very petite young woman by the same name as the woman who'd filled my shoes as Class President for the past few years; who worked as a bartender at the club where I briefly worked. The last time I saw her, she said they thought she might have cancer. (The Best Man).

And the girl from my high school basketball team who wore dresses and pumps to school every day just happened to run into me while I was pan-handling one day a few years ago. She told me that she lived in Southeast and her boyfriend was taking her to the movies. She didn't take the opportunity with me to go to the movies or out to a restaurant. She simply held a long conversation with me after giving me a ride. We just sat in the car talking. Never mind the ignorant people, and the things we can't control. The point is to enjoy your life; right? She's actually a nice girl. I've never seen the movie in its entirety. Is she trying to say that *Juwanna Mann* is about me? Well, in the movie, the actor/actress says, "Jerry, here's one for you too". My mother died the following year. Jerry, is my father's name. I don't think they were speaking about an autograph. I've just recently seen this film, but was it supposed to be a hint as to why I'd somehow, lost every friend I'd ever known.

What could I have possibly done to be shunned this way? I know it must be something they saw on TV or in a movie and they chose to believe that it is accurate information about me. I swear, it's like the entertainment world is the bible for earthly beings.

How is it at all possible that I've lived in this area since age two; had plenty of family, neighbors and friends nearby, while working in a hair salon and planning a trip to California. I didn't tell any female friends or invite any female cousins, and no one invited themselves to go with me. That means I wasn't doing their hair, they weren't calling me on a regular basis and/or they had no desire to even fly over there to visit, with me. (I'm sure my parents mentioned it and it spread through the family grapevine).

For the past 10 years or so, I've only been allowed to have one friend at a time; the length of the friendship is monitored and there's no over-lapping. Whether with a soror, a new person that I meet at work or a romantic relationship with a long lost friend. (Think about what I'm saying).

The bible says to have friends, you must first show yourself friendly. I send messages to many, they just don't respond. I'm struggling here to recollect exciting adult moments with most of these (former) life-long, female friends.

Now these women, some who are related to me and others who were kind enough to invite me and my daughter to live with them briefly during our unfortunate situation, chose not to go out and be seen in public with me. However, even before I became the crazy, homeless lady, these such cousins my age and former neighbors and/or schoolmates, didn't accept my invitation to go bowling or to a movie, to lunch, or to an inexpensive play at the community playhouse. Now if you recall, I've been formally trained in the area of etiquette (for my pageant). I'm not loud or rowdy in public and I didn't think it was painful to look at me. I guess everyone was lying all of these years. They all really think I'm ugly.

I know a woman who has 6 children by three different men. In her late 30s she finally married. She dropped out of college, but she is making very good money as a paralegal and she owns her own home. But the entire world believes I'm 'Erin Brockovich'. What I'm about to say is extremely important. Since I've been homeless, I was hired by a two-man accounting company as an assistant. I was required to dress very professionally and attend meetings in the conference room. I didn't then, nor have I ever worn miniskirts in a professional environment. I've never worn a see-thru blouse anywhere. These men professed to be Christians. One of the men, tried his hardest to provoke me to argue with him, but it didn't work. I left after two weeks. My managers at Walmart picked up where they left off. They finally provoked me, on the day I quit, to curse at them and leave after about 4 months. (This was the last part-time job I'd been offered and/or accepted since I'd been homeless. Soon after, my grandson was born. I shall hence forth, use my degree to write and earn a living). My mind is just fine. Those around me, seem to be losing their minds.

(OK, I had a chance to purchase a home before, but I didn't, because I didn't like my job and didn't know how long I would be there). Unfortunately, sabotage caused me to lose my most recent career right before I purchased my first home. They tried verbal harassment to make me leave. It worked at first; I left. But I went back. I guess they realized they had to come up with another plan. And they did. Yes, I actually asked the high-school students at one particular school why they were acting this way everywhere. He told me that they were trying to make me lose my job.

It was almost as if all the females on this planet had formed a union that I wasn't allowed to join. Now, all of my friendships/relationships from here on out, must now be with males.

I would love to travel and go out with my female friends. On many occasions I recall attempting to initiate an afternoon out with my daughter, my soror, and her son. I recall taking my closest girlfriend from high school to a concert for her birthday. I recall inviting my cousin to ride with me to Miami. I invited them.

This is you all; "Don't worry, we aren't going to let her work in a flourishing career or earn a lot of money. We know how important it is to everyone, (including her former friends and most family members); that she stay in loser status". To prove me wrong; purchase my book. If for no other reason than to support a homeless woman.

I would never have sex with anyone casually. I'm not crazy, slow, or lustful. I've never robbed anyone and I do not steal. I would prefer to hang out with straight, educated, females for an afternoon of fun; rather than males.

I would never call anyone a ho; harassing them at work, and/or in public or private; even if they are my age or much older and have never married and/or never had any children- which is the case for many of my high-school/college friends, family members and most Hollywood Actors up until about 5 years ago (now they're all having babies at 40). Even if they met someone at work and they became sexually active before dating. Or if they meet someone somewhere and have a baby by them before they know if they're going to marry them.

(I'm 40 and I'm being forced to have a baby in my midst for companionship. If that was what I wanted, I would have had a bunch of kids out of wed-lock for companionship).

When I hear a woman say, "You're a ho and we aren't because we wait and you don't"; then I know that they are mentally slow; and mean, and I'm not. (Even if you don't know the specifics; what kind of normal minded adult argues and harasses anyone about their personal relationships, saying "you just want to have a penis in your vagina?")

Hey, Black Girls Rock. Why was last year's host wearing hooker boots? And by the way, everyone; especially Ethiopians; stop saying I look Ethiopian when you see me. Because I don't. Are you talking to the 'girl being questioned on the stand' in Legally Blonde (who looks Ethiopian)? (Is she married in real-life)? Yeah, I'm mad at my father for leaving me homeless. But how would you know that back in 2001, when Legally Blonde was released? What more could I do to be considered a productive black woman, as to not be mocked or humiliated through Black shows? I want to pursue a writing career, independently. But not having friends makes it seem as though, the world is saying, no, just be a ho; loser. **Oh I get it. Just stop me from making any money to create the illusion that all the hurtful information on TV and in movies, is all about me and I'm trying to hide.** I had a husband and I have a kid. It's not too late to have a career unless you are hell-bent on stopping me.

On the other hand, it's a little late to have children at my age. I mean no disrespect; but understand what I'm saying.

I'm homeless and I guess the dark-skinned Annie said it best, my hair is ginormous. I will never be married but I'm not now, nor was I ever, wearing hooker boots.

The 'ironic' part is that my former best friend, the surgeon, is in LA now and has married into the family with last name of the hostess with the big hair.

The first year I actually flew to L.A. was toward the end of 2001, a week before the attack on the Twin Towers. Believe it or not I called the Terrorist hotline with information about something that happened near me in the airport, on this end, before I left.

Chapter 6

My Philosophy on Friendship, Dating, and Marriage

Now any educated person who has experienced true friendship and love at any given point in his or her life, knows that you can't make up the rules of how you're going to fall in love, before you actually fall in love. No, you do not have to have sex for a relationship of any sort to be serious. People meet in many different arenas and develop feelings for many different reasons. But to those who say I'm kidding myself to expect to be dated and married at this point in life, you're the ones who are mentally ill.

If a man says that his reason for sleeping with another woman while in a relationship with you, is because that person was a ho, and the conversation ends there. There would never be a reason for anyone to be committed to anyone else or to be married at all.

I wonder when people talk on dating sites and realize that their potential mate is 30 and/over; never married, with no kids; do they say to themselves- "Well what was it then? Is she dirty? Did she smell? Is she crazy? Did she used to be gay?" Or do they just befriend the person and embrace the love they've found. Oh I see, they were just focused on becoming rich. OK, next topic.

I had a close girlfriend who was living in California when I visited. She hadn't solidified a career, never been married and had not had any children, all because of the time she'd spent helping her man get his career and life's goals in order. She expected marriage but then they broke up. I chose to spend my time getting to know a kind, attractive man I'd met. I was also trying to further my career in another state. I knew I would have time to hang with her. I wasn't being a ho. It's a natural gravitation. I didn't sleep with him; (until a year later). I mean I could, maybe see someone ridiculing me if I hadn't accomplished anything. I am very accomplished. (My divorce really set me back). No, the relationship didn't work-out. No I did not move to the west-coast. But for some reason, she no longer talks to me.

It's baffling that two of my closest, former girlfriends, both who's breast are or at least were; while they were adults, smaller than mine; are now both living in California and are married. The advantage they had over me was that they didn't start out with a marriage and a child, then attempt to play catch up. I already have a life established here. I knew I couldn't drag my child along for an uncertain future on the other side of the world. Had I known that no one here would be supportive, I'd have left a long time ago. I thank God for favor with the police here, if nothing else. I do not believe that distance is the only reason that these female friendships have dissolved. Although I may have considered being a live-in nanny for my doctor friend so that my daughter and I could become established elsewhere, I am not Geneva from *Jumping The Broom* nor am I the person who gets the shout on Black Girls Rock, who is willing to give their child up so he or she could have a better life; we're a package.

A relationship with a man; that has become a friendship first because you've grown up living near one-another, and or attending the same school or schools, is a creature of a different dimension. When you already know each other's families; you know what kind of student the person is; you probably even know a few of his or her bad habits; you're practically feel like family. Sometimes that's a hard position to be in, before you begin an intimate relationship. Do you see the sarcasm in the point I'm making? "No, because we believe you smelled/(smell)."

You might be on a business trip, taking place in another state and meet someone working for the same company. You may spend one week talking and already know that you want it to become a serious relationship. No, you do not have to have sex that week. You don't even have to kiss.

Afghanistan is far and can be lonely if you are stationed there for a long time. No, marriage vows shouldn't be broken, but there are a lot of people there who are single. Yes I believe and understand that fornication is wrong.

When you're homeless and you meet another person who is homeless; usually that means neither of you has another best friend anywhere else in the world. (Unless your family and friends are absolutely nuts. Love your neighbor as yourself). It's not rocket science, it's a commandment. You can't come into friendship or marriage or anything in between, with malicious intent.

When you are 35 or 50, you really may not have 5 years to get to know someone before you consider yourself friends. Those who have never been married and/or don't have children, will see things differently.

A great way to meet men, is through a girlfriend. Her mate has family and friends. But you first have to have girlfriends who aren't intimidated to have you around their man. Girlfriends who hang out with you and invite you places. But when you don't have that, as an adult, you make friends in different places in life. What do you do when that's not possible either?

(*The Blind Side*. Yeah I trained with him. No he was never left outside. My ex-husband lived with his parents then moved into an apartment with his new wife. I guess he needed a white family to help him reach his pro-football goal).

I've vacationed in L.A. alone toward the end of 2001. I met a man who drove me down the California coast to a place called Marina Del Ray; I believe, to have lunch. On a different day, in his BMW as I put my foot up on the dashboard-*The Blind Side* We drove quite a ways to go go-kart racing, (*Guess Who?*). He played pool with me late one evening; one afternoon, took me sight-seeing in Hollywood to see (Mann's Chinese and Kodak Theatres etc.), and on a tour of his apartment where we kissed then I returned to my hotel for the night. He took me to dinner and breakfast several times while I was there. We talked on the phone for a year before I returned in the spring of 2003, when we became intimate.

No man, including him, thought I was worthy of marriage. I was a little torn between him and a guy I'd grown-up near in my neighborhood who'd gone out of his way, to begin getting to know me better. In school he seemed nice but as we dated, something wasn't right. So I took a sabbatical, to venture back to California where I soon realized that moving there and living on my own, was not a reality without a current stable job; which seemed as if it may be a challenge. Moving across the country and depending completely on someone you've only known for one year, is not wise. But my friend from high school had already decided that he felt deceived, upon my return. So I guess I was to blame. Seems very similar to the situation from *Love Jones* to me. I was completely honest with both of them. But anyway. See, the uneducated, dumb, ghetto response to this is; "She went to California because she's a ho." I'm being set-up. Something wasn't right about the relationship here. No, the police didn't beat me up in the street without me brandishing a weapon but what I'm dealing with requires the same attention! It doesn't call for you to force me to babysit for free until I die of cancer without income or health insurance.

Now it's my business if I met them and never had sex even after several months of time spent talking; him riding up to the median to give me joint juice to drink, to help me through the cold weather; an hour ride with him and my daughter to a cook-out; a nice drive to a bordering county to take in a movie, have dinner and window shop. Maybe I met them at a car wash and two weeks later we became intimate- {(Seven years later we're still off and on falling for each other). I was getting to know another guy during this time as well; five years. They turned out to be true love impostors. They refused to treat me right}. Please understand that just because our relationship was on and off, doesn't mean I knew the truth about his alleged relationship with another woman. (Five years and seven years). You always expect it to get better. I don't care if you think I'm lying. And literally these were the only two people talking to me on the entire planet. (My daughter was in the crazy teen-age phase of life when the telephone is your best friend). She wasn't talking to me either. (She thought I was crazy). Both of the men previously mentioned, were homeless too; living with family and friends. Both of these relationships are over now and I'm very happy to be single.

And trust me, I've said no to 2 times as many guys as I had actually been intimate with. My breath didn't smell. And I wasn't naked when I said no. I believe 90% of the reason for this problem was due to sabotage; libel and slander; (that prevented me from prospering), not because of the shape of my nose or the way I smelled! Now, my breast are small. I wear a 34B. But you can see that before you ask for my telephone number.

There's one thing that I want you to ponder. The entire time I've been homeless; where are the hundreds of men that I've (lived near) known for decades? Where are the hundreds of men that I've clearly turned down for any type of relationship other than an honest friendship? I've dated plenty of people that I haven't slept with. It's not inappropriate to stay friends with men or woman who you've maintained a friendship with, even after you're married. It's all an attempt to create an image that says, I've slept with every guy I've ever known.

For those who think I'm a player, please realize that I've been dumped by plenty of men, all whom were seeing me at the same time as another big titty, well-to-do, woman that I didn't know about. I didn't even know I was dumped; I was still calling. Oh, now I see you're not planning on calling back. These were not one-nite-stands.

A great comparison to such a situation would be the relationship that I have had throughout my life with my father. In many ways he was a great dad. In other ways, he needed a little guidance. (As do we all). I love my father dearly. I don't really think my father finds it easy to communicate his feelings to his grown children. But I'm not surprised. Blacks in general seem to have a strange way of showing love and concern. (Maybe he didn't realize what my brother needed years ago). I don't really understand why my brother hasn't written me on a regular basis. Maybe I would have had a better understanding of his needs as well. My father has accomplished most of what he wanted to accomplish and then some. He didn't see things the way I did. He felt that he had done enough for me and that I'd had enough chances at a good paying job and prospering. I pray that when I see my brother I will be surprised with good news about his situation.

He didn't ask me many questions when I was young, so a lot went unsaid from parent to child. But The Cosby Show allowed him to sit back and view a not so accurate rendition of my basketball boyfriend from high school, coming to visit me. I remember asking my father if he could come over. (No we did not have sex). My best friend during this time, who looked just like Rudy (In the face), had a high school basketball boyfriend who had the same name as Rudy's boyfriend. The relationship I had with my boyfriend didn't last very long, (probably because I didn't sleep with him), but he did sit next to me at our most recent, (20 year), class reunion. He flew in from overseas. The funny part about all of this is that my basketball coach had a family structure that was much similar to that of the Cosby family and the character who played 'me' was using his daughter's name. No wonder he gave me his daughter's jersey (22), after she graduated.

Although he wasn't a boyfriend, my father is a male and we do have a relationship. Who knows, maybe it was the way I responded to the things my father said but I found myself in an on and off relationship with him as well- ok, not really, but I could only take him in doses. After my separation from my husband, I moved back home. My dad drove me crazy! I had to move back out. (Needed to save money due to a situation on my job or other extenuating circumstances)... Moved back home.

My father has been living over 4 hours away for about 10 years now. When I talk to him, it's because I've called him. I guess that's his way of saying, "I don't need you; you need me". (No different than the other former friends and family members I'd known). But when he's here (which is quite often; or we're there; (which is hardly ever); we have a good time. The best part is that he's saved now; and has been ever since my mother got sick. I know this sounds bad but from the outside looking in, it seems like he moved away just so that my daughter and I wouldn't have a place to live. I know he loves us more than anyone will ever know. Today he is one of my closest friends, even though he left me homeless.

I have gone two years without having sex. I've been in numerous relationships with men without having sex at all. I've been in plenty of relationships where we weren't intimate until at least 6 months; sometimes 1 year. I've been in relationships where we were intimate and then stopped. It was a quest to be mean, to me. My behavior is not the ingredient that needs to change.

My expectations are not low in a relationship. They are actually high. When I don't get the treatment I expect, I assume we are just friends. I'll begin talking to someone else and I will tell you so. And I I'm not a cheater. So this is why I've accepted being single for eternity. Because I now know that men refuse to treat me right. I didn't realize that they were using a specific poem that I allegedly wrote as there reason to say that I don't want nor deserve mutual love; until two days ago. But if we base, deserving mutual love; on mistakes made, there would be no love in the world.

The only time in my life when I'd had a one-night-stand; was after a Howard University Homecoming party. (I would never intentionally have a one-night-stand. And I was set up. Then mocked in a black movie love drama on screen for all the world to call me names. He shared the same (real-life) name as the late Batman character; the joker. (I didn't know the jokers real name until after I saw the movie, years later).

Now I'm homeless and being deceived and lied to, after being left without shelter! So the crazies are going to try to flip the script and make it seem like I'm the one who's crazy! I'm believing that I'm in relationships with honest people who are single! There are people who intentionally get into relationships with people who they know are not available! They're not being harassed! I'm not an un-repented sinner. Any sins I committed while being deceived are irrelevant right now. I commune with the Lord on a daily basis.

So My Grandchildren Will Know the Truth

The four main reasons for this book are; one, to leave an explanation to my grand and great, grand- children as to why they may have issues in their progression in life; two, to express a deep concern as to how and why my elementary school aged daughter and I were separated and left homeless indefinitely by everyone; three, to make known to the world that the libel and slander going on in California against the educated, working class, needs to stop; and lastly, why I am being verbally harassed by everyone on the metro bus, in the grocery store, in the library, at church and anywhere else you can think of. Sounds like the civil rights era huh? You would think they were white or something!

TO: my, children, grandchildren and great-grands; etc.... I've never done drugs and men didn't smell me during intimacy; ok, (Twice in my life). I have never sold sex. I do not have casual sex. There are many other people whom I've dated and did not sleep with. Every guy who I've been friends with, who wanted me to be their girlfriend but I chose to keep it at the friend level, stopped being my friend. I have had sex with more men than you read about in this book. "Well when did you sleep with those people"? Not in college, not when I was homeless. When I was thriving. When I was newly divorced, dating and working hard; with my own place and car. The perfect time for me to date and look to remarry. So what happened? A bunch of men, some familiar; some new, who were more infatuated with sleeping with the famous TV girl; then embracing a real love with a kind, successful, single mother who cared about them. No matter how long it took to sleep with me. Even if it took 15 years. As you can see in my first relationship out of my marriage. No I did not know this then. I hadn't heard the songs of sabotage. I hadn't seen all of the slanderous movies. And even if I had seen a few movies, I didn't see them the way you did, because I knew it wasn't true. Think about it. Do you realize that when I watch a movie, I'm not looking to see if I'm being talked about? I just laugh, or cry or plug my ears. Sometimes a movie may have been out for years before I watch it a second time and see it a different way. But then I'm thoroughly disgusted about the insinuated lies. But what more could I do but let it go and move on with my life.

Speaking of moving on with my life. Grandson, I loved you more than you will ever know. I wanted to continue to babysit you but my life is at stake. If your father stays with me at the hotel and quits his job, maybe he can watch you but other than that, your mom will now have to find a daycare provider for you. They refuse to pay me. I have decided to go back to the hotel and panhandle full-time. Tuesday, May 5th, 5:18am. The entire world has formulated lies about me and convinced themselves that they are true. They are literally trying to kill me. I am not paranoid. There is a hard lump in my breast and every time I hold you up against me, it hurts. That's never been the case before.

I'd never had sex with two men within 3 months until I became homeless. I had sex within 1-2 weeks with my 5 year relationship mate and my 7 year relationship mate while I was homeless. And it wasn't for money. I've never initiated a fight and never hit anyone back who hit me in the mist of their craziness. If I'm crazy, I would be crazy all the time right; everywhere? (Unless It's a different personality. I do not believe I'm schizophrenic). People think my daughter sold sex and has body odor. She doesn't. Although, some of the clothing she chose as a teen-ager while away from me, was not befitting for a decent young woman. **(I admit I've made mistakes in relationships; but not very often).** Hollywood wanted to use me to make a point. (For example: Sister Act II; I didn't need to be told to pay attention in school. I've always paid attention and gotten good grades. Oh, the actor/actress meant, pay attention to the movie. Everyone is going to dog me, no matter what. **I don't see myself as a failure, but everyone else does. And they are hell-bent on keeping me down. If by the time I've sold this book, I'm a millionaire or my life is back on track (bills paid and I own a house and a car, then you will know I'm wrong. (Or God helped me find an honest way to get through it).**

I'm one person but I could put information in this book to sabotage someone with whom I hold a grudge. That's not the purpose of this book and that won't give me peace internally. Yet there are those who don't understand why I feel I've been sabotaged. They ask; if you didn't smell, what was the reason that your relationships didn't work-out. Even after reading about all of this sabotage. I'm quite sure that the only reason no one called Child Protective Services when I lost my job and had custody of my daughter is because I may have actually gotten a good paying job. I suppose the woman in *Set It Off* and the one in *Good Deeds*, is supposed to be me. All lies. Even though it's not about us; does the making of the film; No Good Deed, signify that no one was going to be sent to help us?

So if every woman married or not, with whom my daughter and I have lived during homelessness, decided to decline my offers to go bowling, to a restaurant to sit-down and eat, to see a $6 afternoon play or to take our kids out together for the day and the only one who decided to go out with us, took us to a waterpark so that her husband could see me in my swimsuit; does this statement say that I'm not going out because I'm a ho? Now remember, I'm still going out with men during this time.

Not having sex. But I'm just not allowed to go out with the only one man who offers me shelter when I'm sitting outside. The women who made sure that I didn't have anywhere else to stay, are the ones whom these men want to be married to.

Just a side note. A former basketball teammate from high school made it a point to seek me out while I was homeless; to tell me that she lived in Southeast, DC and that her boyfriend takes her to the movies. (I'm sorry, we happened to run into each other). Mind you; she is pushing her late 30's without a husband or any children. She didn't take the opportunity with me to go to a movie or to a restaurant, she simply had a long conversation with me after giving me a ride. Yes, we sat I the car talking. **Never mind the ignorant people and the things we can't control. The point is to enjoy your life; right?**

If you ask me why I believe a woman would go along with having sex with a man whom she loved in a parked car or on an elevator, I would say, she wants to be spontaneous and adventurous with her man. I would never say, "she's just a ho". But, why would a man try to get a woman to be spontaneous and then change their feelings toward them? The entire world is OBSESSED with me; period. (No I've never had sex in an elevator or in a club.)

Periodically people would ask me who was my favorite musician? It was difficult to choose a favorite musician because there are so many great songs that keep me singing as I stand on the median in finger-tip freezing weather. However, there are also those who've made music that remind me of the bad things in life. God says to think on the good things. That was part of my prayer every morning and so the encouraging songs popped into my head. I don't buy the negative music but I can't seem to live in a normal world without somehow finding out that it exists. Homelessness isn't a normal life, and I didn't know about the negative music that everyone believes is about me. (I don't really listen to that kind of music). Unfortunately, finding out that it existed, came way too late. Every black person who isn't me, hangs onto these artists every word, and it has created a fog in their minds regarding the truth about me and my life. But black men chose to pretend that I was actually beautiful, kind, clean, smart, independent and outgoing enough to love anyway even after hearing the songs; when all the while they believed the mess they'd heard. These black men I'm speaking of were men who didn't choose me even when I had my own place, my own car, a decent job, a supportive family, a college degree, a trade license, and a means to vacation by myself. Most of these things still apply. Now I'm homeless, friendless and unemployed. I pray that the education that helped me write this book, will also help me to sell it.

I'm thankful to those who tried to kindly broadcast to the world that all women want love. Those who'd hurt me intentionally didn't, and still don't, care. So much pain they've caused not only me but my daughter as well. I'm not single and unemployed because I smelled or because I'm crazy. It's difficult to pin-point a single reason why life seems to collapse around us at times. But now, years after all of the relationships that should have transpired into forever, are gone, the region where I live can sit smelly people next to me on the bus, they can make the shortest line in the store; the one with the smelly person in front of me and they can even start a rumor that my breath smells; I know the truth. I don't wait until my sanitary napkin smells, to change it.

My breast weren't too small to have satisfying sex; but apparently even if it wasn't satisfying, it was worth a try to quite a few that used to be a part of my life. I've had a lot of jobs that have allowed me to provide shelter and a car for myself. The mistakes I've made at work and throughout my life, are not the reason why I am now unemployed and why I'm being harassed. Life was consistently normal and I was very independent. I don't need to refresh more; I need to enjoy my life more. Nobody can survive in this world alone. I've always known how important it is to have friends.

Before they; (parents & children), made me lose my job, my hours were cut drastically and I ended up using a good chunk of the insurance money I'd received after my mom's death. It wasn't a lot but it could have made a big difference. Had I been focused and not out of my mind with **grief**; grief that unfortunately didn't manifest itself into tears until years later; I may have been able to start a prosperous business that would have brought in significant income. Unfortunately, I needed the money to live on. What everybody thought was help, was driving me crazy. I've been **dangerously conditioned**. Even though our family may have a history of some mental illness, the issue that I was dealing with was coming from an external stimulus. There are other people who have mental illness that aren't in my family and those who just choose to be idiots. I know grief and I know **blatant harassment**.

I was used to being self-sufficient. I signed a lease on my apartments without a co-signer or room-mate. I gave up my apartment before I lost my job. I was around age 34. That's not too old to be purchasing your first home by yourself. I had two PC computers in my apartment. I actually had begun working on my book as I peered out of my semi dirty, balcony window. If I hadn't been forced off of my job, our lives would have progressed in a seemingly normal fashion. (But a stable residence after I'd lost my job, would have helped as well). Everyone thinks I'm just dumb and crazy. I don't even own a business with all of the knowledge that I have. When in actuality, if they weren't so dumb and crazy, I would be able to work! (Hair clients constitute my own business).

I've never needed a co-signer whenever I've purchased a vehicle. Maybe I was favored because my parents had great credit. My ex-husband made a mess of mine, but I had finally gotten it straight. I traveled to New York, Florida, Atlanta, Delaware and California without the funding of a mate. And I paid all of my own bills using a paycheck. Now my daughter, even working two jobs, can't purchase a new car without being asked to provide a co-signer. My credit was great (until I lost my job). All that sacrifice and revitalizing I'd done. My credit was in ruins once again. The only family member willing to take us in and allow our mail to be received in her home, had worse credit than mine. That's been the address on my driver's license for years. Well, she used to until our social circle supported her by purchasing her personalized cakes;

just a hobby. They would buy a cake, but wouldn't come get a roller set or wash and blow dry from me. Since I need ministry. Come get your hair done and minister to me.

{While I was sleep, you know what I dreamed about. The fact that the family near me, can't or won't keep us. And the family far north is on the other end of a tunnel. The family far south is on the other end of a tunnel as well. When the others moved away, they flew. I don't fly..........Those Jerks. (I mean, I made my family disappear). Now I just need a bed in a big house, to jump on.}

Not only do I not ride through tunnels. I can't ride on a super-packed metro buses. If the aisles are crowded and I'm sitting down, I can't stay there very long without feeling claustrophobic. I end up standing for the rest of the ride. I really need a car. Can you believe that people would randomly pay off Christmas lay-a-ways but not student loans. I sure wish some random guy would buy me a car. And not for sex. But because he was led by God.

The one time that I allowed my boyfriend to live with me after my divorce; I mistakenly posed for a nude picture in our living room. He used my camera and it was my idea. I accidentally sent the roll to processing at CVS. (That's how long ago it was; no such thing as a digital camera). I was very skinny but my hair was wet and my hair was sorta long. He wanted to marry me. We got pregnant but I had an abortion; (my only abortion ever). He deceived me and I didn't like it. (Not with another woman). I broke up with him.

If I had a problem with staying committed in relationships, then I would simply say, I have problems committing. That is not an area where I struggle. Life is too short as it is. Why would I cheat in a friendly, romantic relationship?

Oh my God, I almost forgot. I definitely need to explain to them how and why I ended up stuck, for about 30 minutes, in the psychiatric ward of the hospital in my town. It was a complete miss understanding/sabotage. I've never been suicidal. I just had a question for the doctor. I didn't know that if you have a question and want to talk to a psychiatrist, you had to be admitted. I didn't know that the door locked behind me when I was talking to the nurse. I told her I wasn't trying to admit myself but I was stuck at the hospital without any cash and no way to get to the other side of town. Buses had stopped running. You can't even walk away from the hospital because you have to cross a highway. I thought doctors were supposed to be wise, caring people. They offered to bring me something to eat so I waited for the food. It was part of their plan, I suppose. I eventually asked them to let me out. It's kind of like the scene in *Why Did I Get Married*, when the actor/(actress) couldn't get up the mountain so the authority at the time suggested that she sleep on a bed in a (jail) cell until morning. (My speech wasn't fragmented like hers when I spoke and I never had to sleep in a cell). I can't believe they would actually open a file for me in the psych ward. Not quite like Gothika or Terminator but Oh My God; the doctor wanted me to stay in there. I stopped by and formally requested that they send me the report. It was never sent. I shall return one day soon to see what they have on file; if anything.

The entire world seemed to be against me. Buses were leaving me on purpose even if I was running. Sometimes they would ride right past. It was like the Spider-Man movie. My brother used to be late to school a lot more than me. I think that guy in the music group who went by my brother's middle name, was trying to remind him of 'the time'. And that brand new dance called the bird; well I don't believe me nor my brother lack finesse or personality. Saying Hallelujah definitely helps. I hope it helped him.

The people at the subway station yelled, you're going to be late today! The bus driver made me late on purpose by pulling off from the curb at the station later than he was supposed to. It wasn't a coincidence. One time I was left by the bus and was so mad that I began walking across a major part of Central Avenue before I realized that there was no shoulder. I almost got flattened by a tractor trailer. I had to jump up on the slanted part of concrete under the over pass where the truck was coming off of the beltway merging into Central Avenue traffic. There was nothing for me to grab. I think God was holding me in his arms.

And then there was the stalking charge (probation before judgment), that I received for allegedly phone harassing a guy I'd known for ten years. (My, *Day After Tomorrow*, love). I'd just become homeless way out in Waldorf and needed SOMEONE to talk to and to give me a ride back into town during the evening and on the weekends when I had business to take care of. After being indirectly fortunate, yet forced, to live and watch the immobile, ailing mother of a former hair client who lived way down in Waldorf. She; my former hair client and now my keeper; stayed in her room the entire time we were there. Everyone else was at work or school during the day. She didn't even show me before she went to work. I'm not a nurse. How was I supposed to change her pamper? I didn't feel comfortable doing that. Maybe had she done it with me before she left, I would have felt more comfortable. During this year, my daughter caught a ride into town with them so that she could attend the same elementary school for 6th grade. They had a son who had just entered high school. He was kind.

I'd worked my way up as a management trainee and I was preparing for the assistant manager test. He was training me and helping me study. I was standing with my back to him, going through the training system on the computer. When I turned around, he was all exposed. I really liked him and I didn't do the right thing. I remember my former high school best friend saying I need to work my way up. I had no idea what she was talking about until this moment. It's not like I came on to him. I just thought; love.

Ten years, (and a few days of stormy weather) later; I had just become homeless. My daughter and I had been shipped way out to Waldorf to live with my former hair client. My homeless boyfriend who lived with his uncle and sometimes his grandmother; or should I call him my, '7 year on/off relationship friend', refused to drive out to see me for weeks. Then all of a sudden he refused to answer the phone. Even though I lived with her, she stayed in her bedroom the entire time. My daughter and I slept downstairs. He came to pick me up. He wanted to help me look for a job. It was late in the evening but he said he was no longer with his wife. After the man finished buffing the floors; he and I were the only ones left in the (small) building. Yes, we 'made out', in his office. *The Day after Tomorrow*. And yes, it was storming outside. It wasn't a casual thing to me. (It wasn't a one time; random situation). People change their minds all the time about their marriage partners. He flew out of town and when he returned, he called me from the airport. I told him I couldn't sleep because my daughter was with her dad and my client's husband was running a music studio with singers in his basement. He got me a hotel room then headed home to get some rest. Not to say its right. But it happens. (OK, so sometimes we need to rebuke the devil and stand our ground for what we know is right). I guess it's hard to know what's right, especially when that person is your only friend that particular year; literally. Unfortunately, people lie with ill intent and make-believe feelings. Long story short, we aren't married and he's not even thinking about me anymore. And no I didn't' smell! I'll just say, it didn't work out. I guess it just wasn't meant to be.

She didn't really talk to me much; instead, she kept yelling the name of a particular former male friend of mine, when she finally decided to walk around the house. I kept thinking to myself, how could she possibly know him? And who is she talking to? She was at the top of the steps and I was in the basement. I decided not to go upstairs and approach her. However, later that day, I called his office. He and I used to work for the same company. I called the company to see where he was. Of course; right in that same city where I was now located. It's all her fault. Now I had a criminal record, after 30 years without one. (I was so nervous, mad in front of the judge. I admitted to violating the order. She did her job; I didn't go to jail but I didn't do it. She said, "She's a single mother your honor". But more importantly, I didn't realize I was harassing him until I received a paper from the sheriff. (I never harassed him but I did violate a peace order). I simply called to ask why he would get cops involved instead of just talking to me. I didn't even realize I was breaking the law. I wrote every law official and politician, judge and pastor you could think of to make clear that I was claustrophobic and didn't realize I was breaking the law. (This made finding employment literally impossible until I had it expunged three years later.) The strange part is that on three separate occasions he seemed to intentionally show up in the same area where I was pan-handling so that we would run into each other. He was very kind. He was, almost too kind to have not so long ago filled an order against me. He initiated a conversation with me each time. It was as if I had been used to prove that the law had a flaw. How could someone just decide that I'm harassing them by calling their phone and then have the police to show up at your door with a stay-a-way order? There are women in other states who are being beaten and have issues with getting a permanent order to keep a man away from her and/or her children so I understand the need to be able to get a peace order easily but what about people like myself. A peace order just out of the blue? (This is the guy from the make-out scene in *The Day After Tomorrow*; you know after the guy with the floor buffer left). There was a measure of love in the midst. (Even if it was a false sense of love because they were pretending). Even during homelessness. I have never sucked anyone's dick for employment or shelter.

Like most humans, I needed money. I didn't sell weed. Decided not to study the hot-wiring of vehicles. I decided that robbing a bank wouldn't be a very good idea. And no, I didn't sell my vagina. I just asked people for the money, with and without a sign..... And I prayed a lot. With a steadfast attitude, I made pan-handling my new job. But I first wrote letters to the police chief and a lot of politicians about this particular situation as well. But I didn't write the new black, female States Attorney who shared my first name and his last. I definitely should have. At the time, I didn't know of her.

Even after all of this, citizens couldn't let this situation go from their minds even if they wanted to. (Even if it were never in their minds to begin with). I'm a free nanny to my grandson and he and I watch a show about a nanny and a man who shares his name; on Disney channel. How do you praise God each Sunday and pray for your needs while continually judging me?

I want you to understand that as I walked around pan-handling, men would ask me if I had a boyfriend. I would say no. If my man were to ask me if I was his girlfriend I would say yes. This must have been the philosophy that my past mates adopted during our relationships. Telling me yes but telling a new comer, no. I thought I did have a man, but since he wasn't treating me right, I held on to the only friend I had for the past 5 years and hoped that I would meet someone else. Preferably a straight, kind, woman.

We weren't left homeless because I was angry. I'm angry because we were left homeless. As I stood on the median for the last time, right before the cop frisked me and threatened me with hand cuffs, I saw a funeral procession ride past. At that very moment my older cousin was being buried in Atlantic City. She shared my grandmother's name and my birthday. She didn't have cancer, she simply had a weak heart, like my grandmother. They had 13 kids between the two of them. My cousin had to wear oxygen at all times. She was in love and she was happy with her family. I didn't see her much after she got married and moved away but all I have to do is close my eyes and I see her standing next to my mom and the rest of my family; smiling and praising God. I thought about her when I saw the movie *The Fault in the Stars* for the first time. (I'm sure I'll see it again). Now I woke up at 5:00 am 2 days later to type this. Not because I'm slow. Because I chose to do so at this time. (I have to say this because I'm being watched). My mother's voice was on; my father's voicemail message many years after she passed away. It said," You have reached Jerry," (she made the voicemail message). She believed that they killed her because her and my father forgot about my brother. But he is the one who put him out for being a bit lazy. He had to ask him to take out the trash and cut the grass and stuff like that. She knew he wouldn't know how to change the voicemail. The surprise letter that she received was from my mother. She left it our computer in the house for me.

Although I speak a lot about sabotage, I know that more than the countless acts of sabotage you may hear; the heart wrenching part is the lack or female networking, (business cards that were given to me for show), and the decision of those in my circle, to leave me hanging, in my time of need. But God must have been using someone, I'm still here and I'm encouraged. Even though I've clearly being held down by my own people, who were clearly being used by Satan.

I accepted the fact that no man wanted me, a long time ago. Didn't know why and still don't, honestly, but I accepted it. Instead of females befriending me; men who'd been in jail, not in college; men who smoked, did drugs or had wives, were sent to me one by one to apparently help me lose brain cells and entice an audience of Angela bashers. I just wanted to earn an honest living and enjoy my life. I never tried to stop anyone else from living their life. And if after reading this paragraph you somehow think I'm a ho; there's clearly something wrong with you.

The reason why my 7 year on/off relationship has never gotten to the point where it should, is because he knows that we both love each other and he's trying not to date me. (When you come into a situation, with ill intent, nothing good can come of it. No I didn't realize it. In the beginning, I did not cheat. Once I realized it, I let go. But when the entire planet has planned this situation and I'm left without anyone else to talk to, he ends up back in my life again. Usually, initiated by him. I'm sorry, it's not me; I was set-up from the start. The free time I had, turned into; I have to stop past to see my parole officer. OK, that took longer than I thought. Or; Go hang-out with my grandma in the kitchen while I move this furniture out of the bedroom for her. Don't get me wrong, we spent our time alone in front of the TV occasionally. But we weren't growing as a couple. How does that make me a ho?

I never remember saying, dag, my boyfriend didn't buy me anything for my birthday; yet every birthday in my life has been phenomenal. My mom made them phenomenal when I was younger and now I make it a point to be sure and enjoy my day. And not by having sex. I never remember saying; my man didn't buy me anything for Christmas. But most of my Christmases have been pleasant; even while I was homeless. The few that were not, weren't pleasant because I had no money to get my daughter what she needed or wanted. But we had each other. (The money I'd gotten pan-handling was just enough to pay for the hotel and to buy groceries).

Chapter 7

Discreet/Blatant Libel and Slander

From 1984 – 1992, this show aired on mainstream television and if you purchased the VHS tapes, this is what the box said: A widower and former pro baseball player, Tony Micelli, takes a job as a housekeeper for a high powered divorced businesswoman, Angela Bower, and her son. He and his daughter, Samantha, move into the Bower residence, where Tony's laid-back personality contrasts with Angela's type A behavior. Angela's man-hungry mother, Mona is also in the mix. (In real life-My mother was a supervisor over a lot of employees but I was the boss at the Ice Cream Parlor at Wild World Amusement Park.)

"Mona is that you", (that I smell)? *Big Momma's House*. So either me or my mother smell?.... My mother has never smelled like anything but perfume. If I had an issue getting rid of a body odor, I would dedicate an entire chapter to explaining that. I've always had a doctor. Why would I walk around with a body odor issue? If I didn't have enough money to buy hygiene products, then I would just ask someone for the money. But there have been so many lies told about me for so long that everyone believes that the truth is a lie.

Speaking of *True Lies*. It's sort of a major coincidence that in this movie, the actor/actress is dancing in her underwear and hills holding onto her cherry oakwood bed poles, just like I did; in my apartment, when no one was there but me. She uses the name Charlene in the film because the guy I was seeing at that time, was married. He came over while I was in my undies. The name Charlene was used because I was *'Bringing Down The House'*. His house. I thought he was available. I would never wreck a marriage on purpose. This is the same guy from, the scene in, *'The Day After Tomorrow'*. No I have never sucked any man's penis while he was driving a car. My brother's name is Carlos and he has nothing to do with it. My codename is Doris. So everyone is pretending that I have a problem. *Fat Albert*. A man by this name used to live next door to us. Yes he was very big and looked just like Fat Albert. My uncle shares the name of the main character who flys the fighter plane to save his daughter. He was in the Air Force and his daughter used to cheer. They used to live overseas. (She is ten shades lighter than her sister).

I was the Ice Cream Parlor manager at Wild World Amusement Park when I was 16. I managed my former friends who are now: a Nurse, an Architect and a Pharmacist. Is the nurse mad about them offering her a long neck-bone, to pleasure herself in *Big Momma's House* and now she's blowing up the hospital in the movie Batman? (My cousin's daughter probably loaned her the school bus she drives as the get-a-way vehicle; (her grandmother's a nurse; but they didn't use her name). Ok maybe they were implying that she needed to season her greens. Is the architect, the warrior; Tygra Thundercat who is able to become invisible to the human eye; because in real life, she's shorter than most of us. Invisible; or lost, like the children in *One Fine Day*. (She's an architect, I'm a single mom). Is the pharmacist mad because they portrayed her; (titling the movie with her first name); as a sexy lady who sings, with a career that is not respectable and now she's the vengeful Doofenshmirtz on Phineas and Ferb? Maybe we'll all team up and steal the moon-(Despicable Me).

Were our roles now Trading Places. *Coming to America* seems to allow Mortimer and his side-kick who shares my first loves, first name; to get back in the game financially. But gosh, how can I be Mortimer when the bookkeeper on the pageant stage is wearing my black leather mini-skirt and my gray suit jacket? How could that be me when she goes by the name of my cousin who has a sister who is 10 shades darker than her? Maybe it's her sister who wants to get her ex out of his clothing, but I've never been aggressive, physically, with a man (at any age). How can it be my cousins when our next door neighbors had a fluffy white poodle and now have a very big house, similar to the one in the movie? He smoked a pipe and used to own an apartment building. (No it was not in a very safe area). How can it be my neighbor when they're using the name of the former college associate/news broadcaster; whom I saw on Channel 2 while at the shelter; as the dark-skinned sister in the movie. She's light in real-life. (Oh, it's a comedy. When I'm not tanned from the summer sun and I have a curly bush, I look like the wild sister. When its winter and my hair is pressed, I look like the light-skinned sister). Well here's something funny. I'm a pan-handler and I'm happy to get the money that jingles, but I'd rather get the kind that folds.

When does Mortimer really get back on his feet? Giving me a $100 dollar bill once a year while I'm pan-handling, hardly counts. Now all the whore-minded people are saying, "That guy she thought was her man for five years while she was homeless, was really paying her as she pan-handled". All I can do is just shake my head. Well, to that I say, I received $80 one year from a former female neighbor and $120 from a random, Christian guy who was representing his men's department. It's truly despicable to say I'm pan-handling for undercover sex money. I've never sold sex in my life.

I tend to watch the movie *Pretty Woman* every time it comes on the TV because it found a way to get my mind focused on the humorous, fairytale type storyline. I do not forget that the writer has used my brothers rare name and my easily identified, clothing and hat from a picture taken on a local cruise and displayed in a frequently shown photo album, in order to get all other viewers minds on us.

Yes, I kiss on the mouth.

No I'm not her in *Pretty Woman* nor am I her in *Stepmom*. But I could be her in *My Best Friend's Wedding*. They all married someone else! But I want to share this analogy with you. For the past six months I've slept on my daughter's sofa; (homeless). She knows that I do not buy beef, pork or unhealthy snacks and bring them into my place of dwelling. She bought our favorite; brownies, but didn't eat any. I'm home half the day, babysitting for her, for free; while she's at work or school. Slowly I picked, and ended up eating all of them after a few days. I guess you could say I had an affair with the brownies. It was almost as if she wanted me to ruin my diet. I guess this is the logic my intelligent girlfriends use as their rational for not inviting me and my daughter to live in their homes. (I would never try to sleep with their husbands).

I can only make an educated guess that the movie Easy 'A', makes the viewer think of me. I've never seen it. But the title alone probably takes the whore-minded brain on a roller coaster ride. No wonder you imagine that the woman lying on the table, drugged in the Batman's movie, is me. Trust me, it's not.

Yes my husband played football and we have a daughter. We did not have sex when I returned to get my belongings after our separation. *The Game Plan*. Everything we had belonged to me. My mother and father were with me. His mother came in with a family friend while we were moving my belongings out; the woman who planned and danced at my wedding. His mother was so loud, rude, crazy and disrespectful. She acted an ass.

I'm being lied on terribly! I see how innocent people end up dead and/or in jail. I'll be just fine without a man. But why would anyone in his or her right mind, ask me if I'm hurt? There are a lot of other reasons to be hurt other than not having a man. All I can do is shake my head. God knows I can't shake my breast, 'they're not big enough'!

Speaking of not being big enough. Remember, I was dumped but I was still calling. Did they feel bad because they thought they were too small when in actuality they just needed to get off of me and usher me to ride them in an upright position? Daddy daycare huh? My cousin was working in a daycare for peanuts but she got her license and took all the children into her own daycare in her home.

So who is it that's 'getting the bunny' in *Daddy Daycare*? (Sure looks a lot like the guy from my 7 year on/off relationship; that just ended). Or the bunny from *The Wood*? (Sure looks a lot like the boy who said I slept with him at age 9). And is this the character from Lisa and Gaspard, the cartoon? Does she have issues with her body emitting gas? Just found out yesterday, this cartoon names two (extended) family members who live in California; (their real names). But I guess they're not the only people in the world with those names. And what about my cousin who also shares the name of one of the bunnies. She has a sister ten shades darker and they used to live overseas. It's a British cartoon. "Could that toilet tissue commercial about finding a cleaner bum be about the young, black homeless lady not wiping herself well? Or does she want us to hook her up with a different homeless guy whose cleaner?" No thanks, I'm happy single.

It couldn't possibly be because of shows or commercials like the latter; that answers the question of, "Well what is it then"?

But when I start counting the dresses in my pictures compared to the ones I see in the movies I watch; those in my garment bag and the ones lying inside my bin, I realize I may soon hit the magic number; 27. (Of course my dresses were much longer. Same color, same pattern, but much longer and appropriate. I've never worn spandex or a mini-dress to anyone's wedding.) The two beige, lace dresses I wore as a hostess in my cousins wedding and to recite a poem in my grandparent's wedding; commemorating their vows, marking 50 years of marriage. My black leather mini dress; my wedding dress & pageant dress, the yellow dress I wore to a wedding reception, my red and white poke-a-dot dress from the cruise, and the gray bridesmaid's dress that I wore in the wedding of my best friend from high school, **(the one time in my life when I was actually asked to be a bridesmaid)**. It's pretty much identical to the gray dresses the bridesmaids wore in *The Best Man*. "well, what's her name?" Oh you mean my best friend from high school. Well, I don't know if she slept with 3 people at one time but she shares the name of that pretty rap artist with the big butt.

I made the mistake of going to my friend's home for a first date after re-connecting 8 years out of high school. He lived kind of far out in the country and I really wanted to see his home. He had just purchased a brand new Cadillac. ("Throw some D's on that bitch"; it's a rap song). The woman reading the poem, is wearing my shirt and vest. (In the movie; not the one we watched but the one they apparently made 'about us'), I'm somehow riding in the back of a taxi cab with my friend from work whose breast are so small, she doesn't need a bra. She's really pretty and her hair is really big; in reality. Well, it used to be. (She shares the last name of the center in Coach Carter who was failing math; I've never failed a math test in my life until I took a lower level algebra math course at Bowie State University; where I was being verbally harassed). *Love Jones*. I don't know how I ended up in the cab; she and I drove to his auto shop because I still had a car at that time. I'm the one who made the omelet and asked if he wanted anything else. He was allergic to onions. Maybe he took a cab to pick up a car he was going to work on. Lol. I popped up at his home one day and he refused to open the door. He was cheating and it was over. The movie was made in 1997. I didn't run into each other again until the year 1999 or so. So what did he empty his refrigerator of every item except those used to make an omelet? I still don't know how a movie made in Chicago, about a girl wearing my clothes and a man coincidentally repeating what I said 3 years later is even possible. Well the clothes, yes, because I wore that in high school (1988-1991); but the other part is a little creepy.

Now the twisted part is that the one with the big breast is in *Jason's Lyric* and she has my bracelet in her hair. She's reciting poetry. I've never had sex behind a house. And at that time, I'd never had sex outside. I don't know who she represents in the movie *Life*. But I know whose name she's using. I sat next to a guy named Jason on a charter bus; a married guy. And nothing happened between us. We were headed out of town for a sporting event; with that same job. You know the job where I made out with my co-worker after hours. (I am no longer able to ride charter buses).

I recall once being so excited about a relationship with a guy that I liked and had grown-up with after spending time with him and his mom, that I wrote him a poem but did not realize what could have been inferred by him after reading it several times, until I had already given it to him. I re-read it and realized why he wasn't talking to me anymore. It sort of sounded like I was breaking up with him. I'd simply chosen the wrong word. It wasn't a letter to North Korea from the US. Thank God it was just a poem. Well, Now I know why he doesn't call me anymore. This was a friend who grew up in my neighborhood who has a very large, monster dog harbored in the basement of the house where he lived alone; now that he and his wife were divorced.

Even the best fall down sometimes. Even the wrong words seem to rhyme....

Speaking of falling...

The house and yard in *The Fighting Temptations*, sure looks a lot like my grandfather's old house in Emporia. The house no longer sits there but we all have hundreds of photos. My mother's sister; the same aunt who took me and my daughter in when we first became homeless; is the aunt who used to pile all of the nieces and nephews into her Malibu and drive us 'down the country' for the weekend. It was really country. But it was fun. It was like having lots of brothers and sisters.

Speaking of fighting temptations; there's a movie called *Crazy, Stupid, Love*. It was released in 2011. I just saw it today, for the first time. It is May 2015. A man is told by his wife that she wants a divorce. She tells him that she slept with someone else. He moves out. He frequents the bar every night, trying to move on. Unknowingly, he sleeps with his son's teacher. He tells his wife that he has had sex with 9 other people since they separated. I told my husband that I'd slept with someone else after he'd shoved me for no apparent reason. I left him. I went to a few clubs alone to dance and I returned home alone each time; sober. I never went looking for a man but I had no female friends because they believed I was a cheater who didn't get their career underway and now lived in an apartment in a low-income area. I had only male company; for many different reasons. I was hurt about my failed marriage, yeah, but I wasn't having casual sex. (I don't have casual sex). And of course I've never slept with any of my daughters teachers.

The last intimate relationship I had ended because, it was confirmed by his speaking and his behavior that something wasn't right. I'd had the last crazy straw that I could take. I haven't had sex since my grandson was born and I do not intend to. He is now 15 months old.

I've never seen the movie 50 Shades of Gray but I assume from the sexual previews, that everyone watching, thinks it's about me. (Anything about sex, people assume it's about me. "Don't go out, just stay in"- this is a statement about this movie). I'll just say, I would never allow anyone to bind my hands. Maybe since they've used the word gray and gray means smart, they'll think it's about someone else. Why would the same people who make such movies and music that they claim is all about me, run from and grab at the cameras of the Paparazzi? Information about me, even since age 9; has not been accurate.

I will never understand how a millionaire could find his or her work rewarding if the outcome hurts anyone but especially if it sabotages an educated, working class parent whose ancestors had gone through so much. Now, there are people who need a good strong voice to guide them and encourage them to educate themselves, exercise and calm down. I'm not one of them. What could possibly be the productive outcome of those who have been given a voice or pen to effect the masses if they spend every bit of their energy trying to convince the entire world that I'm a terrible person? Then in the middle of a movie that you know is inappropriate in the world of civil rights; you apologize and ask if I'm ok like it's a part of your script. Black people don't trip and fall that much in movies.

Blacks don't seem to have learned a thing from the history of our people. Who wants to have to sue millionaires on the other side of the world to claim their civil rights and be able to enjoy their life? My ancestors fought and died so that I wouldn't have to deal with such ludacris bullying and antagonizing drama. Yet the Black starving artists sold their souls and attempted to humiliate me in order to become rich. I am not a menace to society.

In the film *Baby Boy*, the lady owns a gold car, works at the phone company and her boyfriend takes her to work. I then, drove a gold car, worked for the phone company and my boyfriend drove me to work, in my car. My boyfriends' name was the same as the politician who had a very big dog whom he/we took for a walk, not far from the ghetto (in DC) where he had lived all of his life- (Maid in Manhattan). I purchased a gray sweatshirt while I was in California. At some point, back on the East-Coast, it became a missing item in my closet. I waited year to sleep with this man whom I dated while I was there. I made a phone call from his apartment as he pretended to sleep, not far from where I sat. My former esthetician co-workers name was the same as the woman's boyfriend in the *Baby Boy* movie. Only, in the movie he was eating her vagina- and in real life she did my bikini waxes at work.

Just a matter of time before people started to point....... To my neighbors and friends, everything they see in these movies, is true. Yes one of the main reasons why my marriage didn't work-out was because of my husband's temper but I had never in my life been punched in my face, until I rented a room with an alcoholic woman while my daughter and I were homeless. But let the world tell it and I'm a battered woman. (We had two cars but we chose to drive to and from work together every day). (Unfortunately, tempers and violence can lead to death. I'd never seen a temper within the 4 years before we got married). If I may brief you quickly and move forward: His parents were pastors. His mother was pretty much demanding (constantly suggesting) that I wear make-up to church. "Well that doesn't sound like a Monster-in-Law to me". (No, I was just trying to find ways to get out of my Christ-led marriage). `I was working through a temp agency when we first got married. He wasn't a doctor, but my pre-med, room-mate, girlfriend shared our apartment when we first got married. He worked for a stock investment library. He took his mother's side regarding everything. One day I went to hug his father good-bye and he kissed me on the mouth. I was paralyzed but I sort of brushed it off. It was really shocking. My birth father never kissed me on the mouth.

One day on our way to church, I was crying. He was furious at me for crying and not answering him when he asked what was wrong. He seemed to be going into a rage. When we got out of the car, he grabbed me and violently shoved me up against the church wall, before we entered. That was strike 3. I wasn't really counting mistakes but something definitely wasn't right in our marriage situation. I began talking to my ex; my first love. He was a mechanic so I had him do my tires. My daughter was about 5 months old.

One day we kissed and the next time we met, we had sex. (A lot of time transpired between the kiss and a little more than a kiss). Apparently, enough time to make a song. I wanted him back and it was love.

It was almost as if he created and released the song before I returned home: "Where you at, paying car notes, while I'm swimming in your women like the breaststroke; tongue all down her throat. Nothing left to do but send her home to you, I'm through!"....... Was it just a huge coincidence? (After reading his real-life story as well as his surviving wife's; I have to wonder if either me, my daughter; him or his surviving wife, weren't being set-up from the beginning). Whichever came first, the chicken or the egg; I'm not a ho.

(I hadn't grown-up amongst gangs and violence but now my life is being threatened because I'm writing a book about the rumors and lies that ultimately changed the course of my life; and my child and grandchild.) Had I not lost my career due to harassment from that Shark Tale cartoon etc., her permanent residence, (life), would not have been so unstable.

I told my husband about the situation and he again grabbed me violently....I left and never returned. My first-love didn't get a divorce- but I did. I initiated it.. I didn't tell him because of the rap song. No one will ever believe that now. (Hearts break but they don't break even)

Now the entire world believes I'm *Bringing Down The House.* The leading actor (actress) is using my middle name. Her role is not indicative of my behavior at all.

I recall my mother's best friend coming over to our home one day. I was watching the news and talking to my mom while she cooked dinner. She made a little small talk and as she was leaving she said, *The Brother's* Angie. I said, "I saw that movie; it was good". This book is almost finished and I'm just plugging this in. Why would everyone or anyone think anything in this movie is about me? It was almost as if she thought someone was listening and she wanted everyone to believe that the crazy slutty women are me instead of the women that they are obviously portraying. Certain people pop into my mind when I watch this movie because of their eye color, geographic location, occupation, or the way their husbands look. Yet, I would never go to their homes and shout, *The Brother's* girl, that's you. Because inquiring minds need to know, I've never kissed a man and then dated and slept with his son. Nor have I danced in my underwear in front of a man as he sat on the sofa. I do fall short of God's will at times, but I do not make a habit of enticing men; *Cradle To the Grave.*

That's actually one of the reasons why my (high school) best friend and I are no longer friends at all. She would call my phone and before I could get any words out, she would yell, that's you! I eventually realized she was talking about a movie. But see, her father; our boys and girls club basketball coach; was the long-term boyfriend of my mother's best friend. Basically, her step mother. She's the one who came to my house and shouted *The Brother's.* (She was the mother of another young woman on our basketball team who preferred woman. She was the former best friend of my best friend, before I came along. But they're (like) step-sisters).

Let me give you an example of how the information is twisted and slanderous. The only time I've ever been told by a man that I embarrassed him in a restaurant is when I pulled out a coupon for the Olive Garden while dining with a former, life-long friend one evening. This would be the guy that looked like the dark-skinned chunky guy in Brown Sugar who sang, "The ho is mine." (This is about how true the rest of the information is in the movie is, regarding myself).

Remember, after I lost my teaching career and I was devastated. Well, I needed a car. I ended up purchasing a very old, used Ford Tempo like the one in Monsters' Ball. I bought it from my ex-boyfriend who owned an auto shop. I made him buy it back from me when it broke down a few weeks after I bought it. This particular boyfriend graduated from my high school one year before me. He didn't become my boyfriend until approximately 8-9 years later. I made him an omelet at his house the morning after we had sex, remember. He said he was allergic to onions, so I asked him if he wanted something else. (I do not believe I'm allergic to onions was a euphemism for I smell; I did not smell). *Love Jones.* "Let me break it down so that it will forever be broke". A comment from an actor in the movie. Well they broke down what they believe is my information and now I'm broke. My best friend from high school actually moved to Chicago for a few years during this time; before she eventually moved back home. The actor/(actress) was wearing my shirt and vest when she read the poem. Now, the woman with the double D's in the back of the cab, is in another movie and she shares the name of my cousin in Newport. This particular cousin has a sister who is 10 shades lighter than her. And she shares the name of the white bunny in the cartoon about the black bunny and white bunny, who are friends. These cousins (of mine) are both married. My aunt told me that this particular cousin, had two pet dogs. I wonder if she was lying. (That's why you shouldn't tell lies). Oh, the two dogs that got pushed off the bed before the characters in the movie made out? My cousins are both married, so they won't be verbally harassed either way. But I didn't do that, maybe they did it, but why is the woman wearing a yellow dress; in *Welcome Home Roscoe Jenkins*; like the one I wore to my former friend's wedding reception! (The girl in Columbiana has two dogs but she doesn't have double-D breast). I don't think about them whenever I hear either one of their names on TV because I'm not obsessed with finding information about them or anyone else, on television. It's a British cartoon. Ironically enough, they used to live in Europe. I'm not a liar and I'm not pressed for a man.

This is not about being smarter than someone else. This is about others lying and having others to lie for them so that someone else gets blamed. And then the liars shout, "No it's too late to tell the truth!"

The way that someone wrote movies about me so that if I ever told on them, I would also tell on myself; is the same way someone else wrote movies so that you would know that I'm being blamed for other peoples actions. Plenty of wolves, in sheep's clothing; literally. When this happens, your eyes and brain are unable to process who's actually faltering; until 10 or 15 years later when you finally put it all together. By then, their married. The one left single, is the one stuck in your brain; but not necessarily the culprit!

Hollywood Homicide. I could do a full story board of my vacation pictures matching scenes in this movie. Including the Malibu I rented from the airport. No I did not kill anyone. It was actually a very nice vacation.

I worked with a man who shares the same name as the young son in Big Mommas House II-(that's a pretty rare name.) He was one of my two escorts to the company Christmas party. The company where I made out in the office after hours with a co-worker. *The Day After Tomorrow.* No I didn't kiss or sleep with either one of my escorts. And I danced with a completely different friendly male co-worker who would later take me to Tysons on a dinner date. (Yeah the guy I made out with, was there with his wife I'm sure, even though I do not remember seeing or speaking to him. In my heart and mind what happened between he and I shouldn't happen if your marriage isn't already ending for some other reason.) I've never stolen any money or known of such, as they did in the movie. I've never been molested by any aunts or uncles as some vivid imaginations may infer from another scene in this particular movie. (Understand; I didn't get fired from this job. Eventually I put in two weeks-notice. I was fired from a completely different career, 8 years later, after being set-up by the very children who had previously been verbally harassing me about the things they'd seen, allegedly about me, on television. You can call me a ho if you want but my heart, mind and conscience are all clear. Hope you're not praying for healing while judging me behind my back.

No, I never slept with or visited the man from my childhood neighborhood who had the same name as the cop in *White Chicks* but the guy from my neighborhood who looks a lot like the cop in the movie, who invited me to his large, very nice, single family home with a large dog scratching at the inside of the basement door, has a different name. He shares the name with the young singer/dancer/producer who announced to all women to shave their cha-cha. (This was one of two situations where I'd known the guy very well and the first invite out was to visit him at his home). (I'd accidentally broken up with him when I wrote him a poem.

The buzz in the air is that I don't know how to move on when I've been hurt. "Let go; Get over it, you say." My response to that is: Yeah I had sex in a few places that were not in my home. YOU need to get over it! And let me and mine go on with our lives! You don't hear me calling the people on the bus; uneducated whore-mongers for having children and expecting the state to feed them. I don't know their story. I try to be polite to people in general.

She's *Legally Blonde*, but I'm sure she's not the fashion merchandising major who was in charge of contacting the stores in my home-town to make sure I had something nice to shop for in my size. Even though my old girlfriend and co-worker from the spa in Pentagon City, was a Fashion Merchandising major, whose long-time boyfriend's last name was the same as Wilona's. I'm sure it wasn't her either. She lives in California now.

Yeah, yeah, yeah; save the last dance for me, I got into Georgetown. But now you think I'm an idiot for not going. I didn't think we could afford it and I saw roaches on my over-night stay with my host student. Before I went to college, no one asked me why I didn't choose Georgetown, including my parents. (Now who says majoring in Communicating isn't a good idea.) Save The Last Dance; I rode the train with my mother to New York City one time. That's her sitting across from me. I walked through Pentagon City Mall with the young lady who now services all of my esthetics clients. That is her silver puffy coat. No we did not pray as we walked. Yes my friend shares Derricks name in real life and yes, she is a doctor. Yes, I do need to find my brother, as the actor/actress expresses as she leaves the club. And yes, after my divorce, I lived in what my old friends would consider the ghetto. The boom-box can be seen from *Karate Kid* to *Save The Last Dance*. I won it by selling alot of stuff in a fundraiser in elementary school. My father worked at night but my mother and brother were always there at night. Her dark-skinned dance partner looks a lot like my first real boyfriend but we never had a conversation like that, about going to a dance. (Although I played basketball, I wore dresses plenty of times). I decided to go to the prom alone. I guess that's why the writer of this movie decided to say, "All I need to do is find someone to dance with." The actress in the movie whom he says this to, shares the same real life name of my team-mate who went to the prom with another ex-boyfriend of mine from high school. They were sexually active; he and I weren't.

I graduated from Towson State University, where I had been offered a full scholarship. Most of the time I was the only Black student in my classroom. I turned down the basketball scholarship to Salisbury. (Thank you to all of my coaches).

(Did they put me in a host student's room where there were roaches because they didn't want me to choose Georgetown? Was I cast to be with my husband, who was a Blue-chip; prospectively attending school at the University of Miami)? How did we both end up at Towson? Don't know, but it was a great experience overall.

Speaking of being the only 'Black' person. I remember attending a ceremony with my former surgeon friend. She received an award from the school where she studied Medicine. She was the first Black female to graduate in the area of surgery from George Washington University.

It's ironic that an actress who is a doctor in the movie, Why Did I Get Married, is standing at a podium receiving an award; and at a separate time during that same movie, she explains how her friend Angela is smart and when she couldn't get a job in the corporate world, formulated her own haircare line. But she made the comment after a student asked her how she could be friends with someone like Angela; a (real–life) character in the book she's writing in the movie. What is not mentioned is 'why Angela can't get a job in the corporate world.' Could it be because now the world thinks she has to get her groove on while she's supposed to be answering the telephone at work (*Shark Tale*). Maybe it's because she made out, after hours, in an office with a co-worker (*The Day After Tomorrow*)? And the film makers just seem to keep coming up with more creative ways to make us all relive the same incident, in new movies. It's kind of like my black mini skirt fashion faux pas that won't go away. (It wasn't really that short).

In your mind, I'm the insecure, loud, alcoholic hairstylist Angela character from several movies you've seen. I don't have much money so I usually don't have any minutes on my pre-paid. That's an example of how exact the money is that I receive for the things I need, when I'm pan-handling. Think about what I'm saying. But they lead you to believe that I'm a very loud talker who is unable to work a modernized telephone. The funny part is that in real-life, people usually say I speak too softly. I've never once accused my husband of cheating nor have I ever struggled with alcohol abuse. Ask my husband if I've ever had a problem submitting as unto The Lord. The actor/actress has an oddly shaped nose. Not like mine, but oddly shaped. My former co-worker; who has the same name as me; from the hair salon I left when my mother was sick, has a nose like this Angela character. She has two kids; a boy and a girl, and she's married.

To you, I'm the girl who gets clothes custom made from a stylist while my brother walks the streets (of Miami) until his feet get callused. (OK I designed and had made, my prom dress by a kind family friend in the neighborhood. I also had a couple of outfits made for me for the MISS Teen pageant in 1987 by another family friend in the neighborhood. I was crowned Miss Hospitality and 1st runner up. No one makes my clothes now. I'm far from rich). (Yes, my brother walked everywhere he went for a long time because he didn't have a car and yes, my mother surprised my father with a brand new Lexus Land Cruiser in which he chose not to keep because he thought it was too flashy).

And yes I have a copy written poetry book that I began in middle-school. And yes, both of our parents worked for the post office. Here's hoping that I obtain <u>Poetic Justice</u> by selling this (book) and my poetry book, since nobody else wants me or my brother.

Now she was in this movie, Poetic Justice, so I believe that she is also opposed to the violation of my rights. But why would she keep screaming my name in the movie *Why Did I Get Married?* She wouldn't go and make fun of my pageant/wedding gown in the Professor Klump movie now would she?....... Of course not. {And why would anyone want me to lose brain cells, (by not talking to me; in real-life)}? Did I mention that the other shorter woman in the Klump movie, used to date my daughter's father in middle school; in real life?

It's a *low-down dirty shame* that another woman who just happens to look Native American, is wearing my dress and using my name when she plays a role in a movie shortly after my break-up with my husband, in real-life. Golly. Go figure. Now, me and my high school girlfriend went to a cabaret shortly after I returned home from my divorce. I wore this dress when we took a picture that evening. She didn't really keep in touch once her career flourished and mine didn't or could it be because she saw the movie with my name and dress. The lady in the movie kept a baby 380 in her purse. No, I've never carried a gun. Now later you will learn that out of college I was hired with an Architect Firm. At one point in my life I had to file a case against the Board of Education. And this young female, former friend I'm speaking of, was an Architect whose last name was the same as the last name in the most famous Board of Education lawsuit. That horrible day in New York; remembered as 9/11; was on her birthday.

I guess had I actually majored in Education when I went to college instead of making it my second choice I may not be in the predicament I'm in now. *Boomerang* was a good movie. I guess I just saw it as entertainment. They were using my name, again; while wearing my black flair skirt. They were using the name of the guy from my old job that took me on the date to the Rain Forest restaurant in Tyson's. I guess they were pretending that we had sex and that things worked out between us. I actually think I messed this one up. He had a black toe, like the guy in the movie, Mr. Deeds. But I don't really remember if there were other reasons why we didn't continue our relationship but we'd had a splendid time dancing at the Christmas party and a night out in a nice restaurant in Tyson's. It's not like I had been knowing him since Boys and Girls Club. I am not shallow. Maybe had I gotten to know him better before he'd shown me his toe, I wouldn't have been creeped out. No, we didn't kiss or touch in anyway. Maybe that's why the woman with my name, in Why Did I Get Married, keeps shouting his name. He was a good catch.

(Why is the actor (actress) wearing my shirt, and her daughter; who looks like my daughter; wearing my daughter's school uniform, in *Beauty Shop*)? I was a stylist assistant at a very prestigious salon in the nation's capital. The white girl in the film shares the same name of the stylist I assisted. I used a small photo album to show her some of my clients and the styles I'd created in hair school. The actress here tells her sister to take a large 'wad' of money she'd been given by a dude, to go buy herself a clue. (No guy has ever given me a large amount of money for sex or anything else). I'm a pan-handler.

In the movie *Clueless*, You smile and laugh so much that you never think that other people may see the same movie in a different way. Sure those who had trouble passing their driving test, were offended. But the ones being accused of doing drugs are probably more than offended; that's sabotage. But anyway- there was a very modestly dressed, super kind, teacher at my high school with the same name as the teacher with the messy hair and runs in her stockings; a black girl who drove a red BMW; a boy with the same name and nose as the drug- addict, skateboarding guy; a girl with the same name as the new girl who did drugs, (The wedding reception that I went to when I wore the yellow dress), and a girl who wore a black leather mini-skirt and jacket just like mine – who said her birthday was in April. I passed my driving test the first time and (still true today), my birthday's in April. I've never smoked cigarettes or weed. (My brother was running late most morning and usually ended up missing his bus. My father was fed up. He made him walk to school; all the time. My mother was already at work.) I thought about him when I heard the boy say without his parents never giving him a ride to school, he may never be tardy. (We have all made a fashion faux pas as teen-agers; can the actor/actresses please takeoff my black leather mini)? Neither one of these two previously mentioned students did drugs in high school; nor did I. (I'm not the one lying on the table in this movie nor in the Batman movie). When I left for college my closest friend and I took pictures together in my room. (Just like Shaire and Dee; I wore a black flowered hat like *blossom;* my nick-name in college). (I wore those hats then too). And a red, yellow and green striped tam that I believe represents the colors of The Island of Jamaica. So is it difficult for you to believe now, that employers think I 'faked' my grades? I read my text books and I studied with flash cards. I did all of my reports myself. I admit that sometimes in college I typed some information that I didn't site. I almost forgot to tell you that my husband was my number 6 sex partner. (Six was Blossoms best friend. This show came out when I was in college).

Now I didn't even give my own husband blow-jobs so I can tell you that I definitely wasn't doing that in high school. It's a little ironic that my best friend from high school lost her mother at age 3 and the white actor/actress in Clueless shows her deceased mother, in the picture on the wall; her test paper. My friend's mother was never fat. I guess it's all just a coincidence. I never discussed sex with any females during high school. Yet the black actor/actress in Clueless, says her man is satisfied but she is not still a virgin; (done with her hands or her mouth). Now remember, the girl with the red BMW at my real high school is someone else. Not me nor my best friend. Now the real-life name of the black actress in Clueless, is the one shot in *A Man Apart*. But now everyone knows her as Angelica from Six Days, Seven Nights. My room-mate in college played tennis at Largo. I was redently trying to sell my poetry book with pictures of myself. I've been defamed. All of my pictures are of me wearing the clothes from this movie. But none of the information is true.

Many years ago an actress who used to **duet with the late singing artist, Sonny**, made a movie called *MASK*. My ex-husband's is an attractive man, but his head is a little larger than most and if his skin is broken out, it's not a good look. Since our divorce, I was supposed to know that mine was an arranged marriage due to the sabotage or I must now **'share'**, (a man). (I guess they think we are both ugly).

I didn't really understand that in the movie *Brown Sugar*, maybe the other viewers believed that after all of 'my' televised break-ups, "I knew I was going to have to share." This was a statement made by an actor (actress) in the movie. I guess it was a secret about me, kept from me, because I'm still single. Why would I want to share a man?

It seems as if someone wants everyone to know about my intimate situations so they can call me a ho and say I don't deserve a nice looking, smart, kind man who's not poor. Comments like, "I didn't know Nike made dresses" to the woman who now hangs with the guy using my maiden name as a writer, in many movies; is offensive. Having her sit like she's a substitute on the basketball bench, while wearing a dress at a school dance; is even more offensive.

Jerry McGuire was interesting. I'd just broken up with my man. We'd both made Marketing/Advertising a focus, in college. He was a free-agent attempting to get back on a team after being cut from the Redskins practice squad. I'd left my reprographics job in the graphics department of a Landscape/Architect Firm, to stay home with our new baby. No I was not pregnant then but we married right out of college. Yeah we were both free and evidently, we were both falling. My very first date after my separation and yes I was overdressed. We had a lot in common. He still owns his own barbershop. "Oh my God Jerry, I'm freaking out". Are you trying to tell my father what I'm doing because Hollywood's sending guys to pretend they are beginning a relationship with me, then tell them to leave me hanging? I just find it strange that the same woman who was in this movie, cursing; unlike me, is the same woman hosting Black Girls Rock, with hooker boots on.

Or, are you trying to say my cousin wanted them to get her husband home to her from Panama after he was hit with a mortar shell?

Oh, they wanted everyone to believe I wasn't being loyal to my brother and offering him a place to live. Please. My brother knows I care about him. Why make a movie. Why wouldn't another family member that was talking to him, just call me and say, your brother needs a place to live. Can he live with you? Or why wouldn't they take him in; since I'm "crazy".

He was a football player who could have easily become a coach had that been his focus. I was a writer who should have had my poetry book published and sold long ago. Although I did not then, and still do not take birth control pills today, *Cheaper by the Dozen* is not how our life panned out. The intriguing part is that an old friend from high school had expressed a desire to own a convertible Lebaron vehicle like her mother's but in the color red, way back when we sat in class during high school. Why that (old) vehicle was in the movie, is strange to me; maybe not to her and those in her social circle. (I do know that the last time I saw the two of them together, they were kissing really hard in a vehicle in my drive-way). I can only guess that because she is married to my ex-boyfriend from middle school (whom I did not sleep with); they wanted me to know that if I were to move to the south to work for her husband (my ex), in his barber shop or, in our other mutual friends barber shop as a stylist (in North Carolina), that she didn't want any hanky-panky. I clearly recall the young adult actor (actress) saying,"Even though you guys live near me now; I have my own life. It's mine, not ours."........Wow. (I know she's wearing my red and white poke a dot dress and is working at an Advertising agency like I had, but I didn't say that). Maybe they really do believe I'm desperate for a man. Why would I just want to have casual sex with my friend's husband? Enough of that non-sense. (The point here for example: is that my mother was married for over 40 years but it's not right to put her in my clothing and make everyone believe I'm her back when she was 18. It's wrong and it's crazy. And I'm not ashamed of my mother or father in any way.

Now I do know a woman who I once worked with, in Arlington, Va., who was sitting on the sofa kissing her boyfriend the one time I went to her home to visit her. She shares the name of this particular actor/actress in this movie who is sitting on the sofa kissing her boyfriend. *Cheaper By The Dozen*.

Meanwhile, back at the ranch.

Which reminds me. The only soap opera my mother ever watched was *The Young and The Restless*. She didn't start watching soaps until after I left for college. My husband remarried a woman who had the same name as his mother-(in real life); (Nick's first wife-on TV). And 'get this', when I met his parents, they lived on Mary Ridge Drive. Overbrook Productions- *Hitch*. I guess I'm Brook. I definitely wasn't the one keeping secrets before or during our marriage; (as the singer so eloquently states in his tune). We had very comprehensive marriage counseling prior to our ceremony. I was naïve; and deceived. They intentionally withheld the information regarding his credit during that phase of the session. His parents facilitated. No, I shouldn't have assumed that everyone has decent credit going into and coming out of college. I guess I was so busy with things, I forgot to ask about that. But I wonder how he was able to remarry so quickly, to a nurse. He never took time to get himself situated. He was still at home and hadn't tried to focus on his goals once again. Plus, he had a young child.

No, we never made out in a library but when we went before the divorce judge, my husband was late. He ran in late practically yelling, "why? why? " -The movie, *Fool's Gold*. This from the man who had an opportunity to start our marriage over and didn't even try.

We had a really big wedding. A little over 250 people. A big group of my extended family from New Jersey wanted to come so I had to rearrange a lot. But at the end; "the more the merrier." *Clueless*. Sorry Haiti. It didn't work out. (Maybe me and my husband will get back together one day. But my mother did have a big 50th Birthday party for my dad-*Clueless*). When we got to the church, there was a funeral going on. I was really hurt. The women waited in the limousine and the guys waited in the basement of the church. My husband sat in a rusted chair in his all white tuxedo. He had to be rushed to the cleaners. By the time he got back, they had cleared all of the mourners out of the church. Maybe it was a sign.

I knew him for four to five years before we married. Not once did we go to the movies. To a restaurant, maybe once. We spent 3 to 4 days a week, at church. Our marriage would have lasted had he not put his hands on me. The movie *Not Easily Broken* is not about me and my husband. I was not provoking him with words when he grabbed and shoved me. All of these so called failed relationships had nothing to do with anyone being a ho. They simply treated me the way they thought they were supposed to. No matter how good our relationship was, it was not supposed to end in marriage. It's not like we argued. Because they thought I was a cheater or they thought I'd said, "You know I can't commit" like the character whose name in real-life is the same as mine, in the movie *The Bone Collector*.

"But the movie told you; I was gonna be married and you were gonna be the ho. They used our names in the movie and everything". "Sorry, I didn't see that movie".

I guess we both have our flaws. After my husband and I separated, I worked to put myself through hair school. I was fortunate enough to travel to New York with the school to a very popular Hair Show with classes and platform demonstrations. While I was there, I went to lunch with a young man who went to middle/high school with me and now owned a barbershop in the south. We were pretty good friends. When I returned home we spent lots of time talking on the phone and he came up north often to visit his family and I believed, to visit me. We were dating and I believed we were in a mutual relationship. (Yeah, the restaurant Jerry Maguire took her to. Same dress and everything. I was overdressed to say the least.) We eventually became intimate and had sex in his car. (I lived in my parent's home at that time and of course he lived in North Carolina). I went to church with him and his sister. I hung out at his parent's home with him every now and again. I drove down to visit him and we went to the movies and to dinner. He showed me around town a little. He just wanted to see how easy I was? What about forever. Why begin with ill intent; especially with a friend? I had no idea that he had another woman in his life until he decided to tell me that he was engaged to her. I went to see Jerry Maguire by myself. I then called my husband and told him to go see it. He cried when he saw it. But it didn't bring us back together.

I saw *Deliver Us from Eva* and *Bad Boys I & II* and realized that I wasn't the only person who knew about the relationship I'd had after our separation. I also realized, I wasn't the only one who was upset about the break-up of that first relationship. Why everyone thinks that's me in the back seat with my head out of the window in *Bad Boys*; I have no idea. I guess that's what happens when you've been brainwashed. He was being blasted for hurting me. Him and his Fairly Odd Parents. Not that the facts in the movie were true; but enough sporadic information to make you say, wait a minute. One of the many troubling scenes was when the prostitute who was shot in the film, had worn my work-out top. Another actor/ (actress) being shot at, was a DEA Agent in the movie. She had on the swimsuit and sarong I wore while visiting my brother in Miami. (OK, don't shoot me; I know my green-eyed friend who owns a Gym down there, is taken).

My uncle asked me one day if I wanted more children. He was wondering why I hadn't had another one. At the time I was sitting at the dining room table in my parent's home. He had stopped past to visit. My response was. Do I have a husband? Well then I'm not looking to have a kid. I didn't robbed my husband of his sperm. Things just didn't work out. (And at that time, I couldn't even manage a boyfriend) –Cheaper By the Dozen. (And yes there will be a book tour. Lol. I'll just be driving from place to place; in the name of Jesus). I'd gone back to school, had my own place, and I was doing a little lite traveling. But no one wanted to join their life with me. (My credit was kind of messed up during this time-frame).

Another show that my mother loved to watch was; Murder She Wrote. The Actress wore my mother's glasses. The main character's name in real life, was the same as mine.

I've always been a fan of Walt Disney. So you finally removed the intro with the young man riding the guitar between his crotch. (Bringing on the thunder). But it made me think about the Run, Run Rudolph song that states the name of my first love and first sexual experience directly in the lyrics of the song. I do not remember what flight it was but I was traveling alone and the flight attendant told us we had to run to get the connecting flight. Rather it was true or not, it didn't matter; everyone ran. I definitely didn't want to miss my flight. Now it's a scene in the movie Home Alone; playing the lyrics to this holiday tune in the background. (I didn't know they were stating his name until a few months ago).

There is an entire show on your network, mocking the red-head. "You mean D-z said something profound?" says, the second main character.

They are bullying the red-head character and trying to crush me in real life. Their parents seem to condone it. Ironically enough the only person in my life whom I've known by 'the red-heads name' in this Disney show, is a young woman who worked in the same company with me for a few years where I had a few failed relationships with men. (Including the scene from The Day After Tomorrow). (Yup, that same job). I also shared with a co-worker that I'd kissed a woman before. She asked me if I was 'coming out'. I ignored her; I didn't really know what she meant but her tone seemed condescending. Now I guess she said it because she was gay. We continued to work well side-by-side in our office. She never made it a point to explain herself. But I didn't really think about anymore, until recently.

I drove around to my old neighborhood one day and ran into the cousin of an old school-mate/neighbor. We sat in his room talking about me moving out of my apartment because my hours had been cut, several months before. No we didn't kiss or touch in anyway. He invited me to attend her wedding reception. It took me so long to do my daughter's hair and get her dressed that I didn't have time to do my hair nicely. I wore a yellow dress and danced with him during that evening. (The cousin of my girlfriend from my old neighborhood). Yeah we were in a bedroom at one point together but there were no dogs and we never made out. (*Welcome Home Roscoe Jenkins*).

Just a small note for you: a different, female cousin of hers, had two children for whom she received child support at one time or another. She shared with me that she was having liposuction done; and she went through with it. (Yeah, it's a song. She went and got lipo wit yo money! We want pre-nup; we want pre-nup; yeah). The bride and her cousin's names are in both movies respectively; Clueless and Baps. I'm sure the writers must be talking about me, they're just using their names. I wonder if that ever happens, in reverse?

I bet you didn't know that my track team friend from high school was a teacher and now is a cop. She gets her hair done at the salon where I was fired for returning late from break. I remember the first time I saw her there. (She had a baby Louis Vuitton under her under-arm).

When it seemed as if the career choices I'd made weren't allowing me to thrive. I actually applied to several different police departments. A better salary, a stable career, and honor of character. With one department I never went to take the written test. Another department said I failed the written test. And the other department scared me out of orientation after driving all the way to Hagerstown. But even that was mocked in the movie S.W.A.T. (Are you still interested in the position? No, I just like applying all the time) - This was never actually said by anyone in real life. But in real life, I did go out for dinner and dancing with 4 guys from my suit and tie job where I worked for two years. You know, *The Day After Tomorrow*; that same job. Afterward, we all went home, sober and alone. But I had a very big party for my daughters 5th birthday not long after that. Everyone in my family was there. From everywhere.

One day; I met a nice, very attractive, young, foreign man while at work. (That same job). We talked for some time on the phone and got along really well. (No I did not know he was from Pakistan until after we'd talked for a while). Once he said that, the idea of a relationship kind of seemed impossible. But he was so cool. I invited him into my home. He brought me some ice cream and we kissed. Somehow every man, woman and child believed I was the blonde woman in the movie *Barber Shop* and I was harassed from that year forward in the salon). I ended up leaving my job. (I never even mentioned that visit from him, from many years prior; while I was at work). But he sure got a shout out in the movie *Barber Shop*.

Although the spa where I worked in Pentagon City was a nice place to work and I would have loved to relocate to Miami and work at one of their locations there; I made a mistake while working at this one. There was one obviously gay guy who worked with me and he was very kind. There was another guy who was supposedly gay but it sure didn't seem like it. We talked a lot because we worked the same shift. I was curiously wondering if he was truly gay and sort of hoping that he would become un-gay. I shouldn't have done it, but I did. I reached down and grabbed his penis. Yup, he's gay alright. He told on me! I got written up. I don't get written up at work. I was so mad. But I couldn't blame anyone for my mistake.

I worked as an esthetician there for about 2 years. On Halloween I wore my wedding dress to work as my costume. Our store set-up was easy to recognize in the movie. That infamous black leather mini skirt that mom bought because 'she loved my smile'; was worn by the main actor /(actress) in many scenes in the movie *Mean Girls*. The 'mean girls' movie was using the names of a group of 'fly' girls from my high school, in real-life. In elementary school, a very pretty girl got hit by a school bus and had to get pins in her leg. Her leg kind of looked like the girls neck in the movie, after she got hit by the bus. Is it my imagination or did I hear the actor/(actress) say, it's time for some major sabotage?

House 1; it's his face, house 2; his name, and house 3; her last name. We all lived next door to each other for over 30 years. He was the mean, poor guy in *Good Times,* desperate for his daughter to find a mate, in *Coming to America* and now he's a minister in *Madea's Witness Protection* Movie. But when it's all said and done, the male role model in each household, in real-life, was stern enough to teach their children right from wrong; patient enough to teach them love and wise enough to teach them how to make it in a world where you're not meant to survive. Each family raised children who went through pains and challenges that the average, single parented; mean child (in other homes), never had to go through.

My father played a major role in my daughter's upbringing as well. I am very proud of my daughter. She has risen to the occasion. She has not allowed life to get the best of her. She is very determined to become successful. My daughter is a beautiful adolescent who has just had a baby. She has a job and she's in college. Contrary to the things you may see on television. She does not have hygiene problems, she's is not crazy and she doesn't have an issue with getting to work on time; neither did I. She deserves so much more than what I'm able to give her.

The only complaint I have with her is that she doesn't talk to me enough. And a hug every now and then wouldn't hurt.

I've been asked more than once, "Who is my favorite musician and/or actor"? It would be easier to name the ones whom I'm furious with. My mother is deceased and I miss her so much. There is one song that quotes her in a compassionate, loving way; I cry every time I hear it. I'm sure my other family members do too. But this same particular musician must have been trying to redeem herself. Several years prior, she'd released a song about a woman 'going down' now that her man wasn't around. I didn't know that sucking on a man's penis 'was a thing', when I was married, and now I had grown up and begun to give blow jobs to some of my mates (during a few particular relationships). She felt that my husband needed to know. Along with the rest of the world. Why couldn't she have just called him? Lol.

I write poetry, but I don't think I would ever write a poem regarding a rumor about the first time my daughter had sex. You talk about, perverted, disgusting, one track minded artists. Although a poem would be much more appropriate to express my sadness; not a movie with names, jersey numbers and birthmarks on the flesh.

Each name in the credits of the movie *Home Alone*, is so significant it's scary. It's almost as if the credits tell a story. They're telling my mom to travel because they knew she was sick but the doctors hadn't diagnosed her problem yet. They're telling me that I'm Blossom and I could have been with my ex-boyfriend from high school. They are showing me that my first love is the husband character on the TV show Modern Family. They're telling me to listen to a specific person's music and or to turn my poetry into music because I've been cast for a particular role, (the ho role). They were also telling me to go eat everybody. They're telling me that I was very stern with the guy who escorted me to our jobs holiday party, when he was too drunk to drive himself home and I dropped him off. Maybe you think I'm paranoid but I know what I know.

In the earlier part of 2003, my mother was undergoing treatment for cancer, but she seemed to be doing ok (with my father by her side). She wasn't throwing up or anything. That year, she told me I could be anything I wanted. That was when I flew back to California to check out some schools that may have been able to help me combine my careers. I really wanted to make her proud. I landed and immediately received a call from my dad that she was in the hospital. It was a little hard to focus but I continued and returned as planned (the next day). Not even a year later, I heard the song," Come Home to Me Charlene," on the radio. (My mother called me Charlene; my middle name; when I was bad). She seemed just fine again when I saw her. Several months later, that fall, she passed away. The heart wrenching part is that several months later when I went up into my cousin's bedroom, I saw one of the last pictures that she took surrounded by her siblings, and I could tell she was very ill. I saw her everyday so I never noticed the transformation that took place after the surgery. Maybe she should have just managed the pain and opted out of the surgery. Nobody knew. God help us.

In 2004; me, my cousin and my daughter took a road trip down to Miami. It was our vacation and Miami is fabulous, but I chose to go there, to see my brother. He was living with his, then girlfriend (the lady in the swim-wear at the luau in Bad Boys II - not really, just shared her name). (The fully clothed woman at the luau wore my swim suit in Bad Boys I). He was earning money by doing carpentry work, from what I understand. He showed me all of the work that he'd done in their condo.

{(I hear rumors that my brother wanted a ride home? I didn't know that. Would have been fine by me. But now I'm shady; for so many reasons?..."Comin From Where I'm From"-video)......And the crazy part is, the boy that I told you about who started the rumor about me sleeping with him at age 9, looks just like this musician}.The video is not true of my life!

I didn't realize, until I went to Philly briefly during the summer when I was homeless, five years later; that my cousin and his wife had a luau every summer. This was one of the 3 places I stayed while in the

Jersey/Philly area. My first Luau ever.

Several years before I became homeless; in 2005; I recall a day that stands out in my mind. In my own apartment; just she and I; we started our morning as routine as any other day. Like any other day except for the fact that I was now working for a salon that was a part of a chain owned by the same company, all over the country; under three or four different names depending on the state. I usually dropped her off at school and proceeded to this salon where I worked as a licensed hairstylist. We were in a hurry and I gave her a breakfast plate while she sat on the toilet. When I got to work, someone knew what I had done. It was like that movie, *Runaway Jury*..... Absolutely speechless. I consider that harassment too; in addition to the other harassment I had to endure while there. The first sentence spoken to me when I walked in to begin working was, "Girl, he did you wrong".

I was being verbally harassed so I took a break but I didn't return on time so they fired me. Now I couldn't work at 75% of the salons in the United States. Weren't they listening to the radio; "Can't Let Go". No matter what the people say they were supposed to love me anyway. That wasn't going to happen now, because this musician had already made them believe I was 'shady'. (It wasn't true but everybody believed it).

I hesitate to think that this tiny thumb drive I'm using to save this document and keep hackers from deleting my words; is the chip given to my daughter to swallow and use as a passport out of the country before she decides to become a serial killer; like the 32A chick in Columbiana. (Note: My daughter wears a 34C).

I know you're saying, 'just calm down'; Maybe *Kangaroo jack* and his fellow bullying crew from 'Hollywood Elementary', had no idea that a prerequisite to becoming filthy rich and famous, meant making their premier movie project (or debut album), a subtle, but vicious intent to insinuate lies and bad mouth me. This movie is not about me, but they are talking to me. They are also mocking a conversation from the airplane ride me and my brother took to Florida when we were young. My ears were popping and I was crying because it hurt. He wouldn't let me get up and get my gum. He got it for me. No, we didn't; nor did I with anyone else, have sex in an airplane bathroom.

I want money! I'm earning it. There was a news story about a beautiful family: husband, wife and three kids; including a newborn. A random airplane fell on their home during the holidays; burning to death, the mother and the two youngest, including the newborn. That's the kind of thing that needs to happen to people who make movies like Liar Liar etc; attempting to, and succeeding in making the entire world believe that I cheated on my husband 7 times and then wanted custody for money. (Not really; but I'm just saying). My mother loaned his ass $6,000 to pay off bills that he lied about before we married. He was violent toward me and I left. I would never have left my husband; even through the crazy antics of his parents. I'm not a liar and I'm not a whore. That punk rock hair-do was just me messing around but my in-home nail technician wore her hair like that to work. Anything that takes the attention off of your face? She has a very dark, large mole covering 1/6 th of her face. And to all of those who see me when they watch the movie, *I Think I Love My Wife*; get over yourself. I never did anything of the sort. (Yeah, the part about the reference wasn't edited out this go around).

The unthinkable behavior is that of the stars who get offended when a lie or rumor is told about his or her family structure or relationship. The first thing they do is wage an (unorthodox campaign: concert or inappropriate announcement to prove that they are legit and that everything the general public sees on TV or in their music, has been about me. Which can't be farther from the truth. You arrive in Hollywood, steal my identity and then use your 'superpowers' to spin information the way you choose to. I see why God said it's hard for the rich to get into heaven. What's going on in your hearts? You can tell me that it's too late for me to say this now if you like. That's fine. How did the actions of those in Hollywood, affect my life regarding the mistakes I made early on; did my life get better or worse? Whose world did you change for the better; your own?

It takes a year to make a movie. Beverly Hills Chihuahua came out in October 2008. I lost my job during that exact timeframe. What, they needed me to fit the script? The dog is living in a cardboard box on the street. They're even using my name throughout the movie.

Do I somehow get picked up off of the street and accept an envelope full of money. Could it be true? (According to this book, I've been in a lot of movies. But where's my paycheck)?

This apartment is not in my name. However, I have been here since October; it is now almost May. I have had one visitor. My father. If my daughter were away at college, she would be a visitor as well, I suppose. I have no phone and no car. No one has initiated contact with me on Facebook. Now doesn't it seem quite odd that I have a grandson right now? If I didn't have him, I would be somewhere else, probably. I'm being held captive. Married people don't believe they can sin. They sin every day. In every other way. (Including the initiation, and spreading of lies and rumors; not to mention leading single people to believe that they are too available). If this were my apartment, that would mean I probably have a job. I would only be allowed male friends. I have had a lot of apartments. No mice running across the floor; no roaches, taking over the kitchen when the lights off. I do recall in one of the earlier apartments when I'd first moved out after my separation; I had a Dancing Feet party. I was a Dudley's Foot-care Consultant out of Cosmetology school. A handful (about 4) of my female friends came over and I washed and groomed their feet. Yes, I'm licensed to do hair, so usually my hair was very neat, if not done in a style. (Well why doesn't she do hair to earn money)? You already read it. They refuse to support me. Christians and non-Christians. Now, the claim is that I smell so they go to someone else. From 1997 thru 2011; I smelled. I positioned myself in a salon at least 5 to 6 different times during this time period. I must mention; that same soror who helped me move my belongings to storage, was formerly a hair client. I stopped doing hair.

'One client is not going to suffice'. I apologize; I failed to mention that she and I went to an event at the Kennedy Center years ago before I'd become homeless. What an adventure. I don't ride elevators and they keep the stairwell locked. I had to be escorted by security through a very narrow, gated stairwell. It was terrifying.

Being homeless is not just about where you sleep. When no one talks to you, you literally lose brain cells. Although my aunt had a home, worked in a dental office, shared the name of the actor /(actress) in Diary of a Mad Black Woman, probably had a lot of ancestors from this place where she vacationed- (Hawaii); and recently passed away from complications of dementia; I feel that my short term memory loss and numerous first dates put me in the running for supporting actress in the comedy, *Fifty (50) First Dates.* Especially since the main character in (50) Fifty First Dates, shares the name of the character in the new movie entitled, *Home;* the most important thing to a homeless person. See, her patients couldn't talk to her and EVERYONE in my social circle chose to stop talking to me.

Remember in the movie, the father and daughter were in an accident. Well, my dad broke his ribs in a 'real' car crash and I hit my head extremely hard when I fell off of my bike and hit a ca. I have short term memory loss. I'm not sure if the bike accident is to blame or the lack of stimulating conversation from other human beings.

So, when the guy with the fast mustang, whom I worked in the same company with for almost two years, took me to dinner in Tysons and we didn't kiss or touch or have sex in any way; was he one of the 50 people I was supposed to sleep with or only date once? When the man who drove me to Arundel Mills for dinner and a movie, and we didn't kiss, touch or have sex in any form; was he one of the 50 people? OMG! What about the guy who invited me to go to the movies while I was standing on the median with my homeless sign. There was a hurricane on the way but I wanted to go out so I went to a movie anyway. We made it back just in time. We talked a few times but I never saw him again. Was he one of the 50 people? I told you I could only date people I wasn't attracted to. That's the rule.

Remember the last 5 year relationship I had where I left the home because I wanted to date and spend more time together out of the home; even though we were playing a lot of board games. I had no one else to talk to or get a ride from so I ended up talking to him again until he decided to stop talking to me so that I would be forced to talk to someone else. Remember the situation and the someone, that ended up being?

If they weren't able to steal my script before it was filmed, I swear, I'd write a movie myself. They're spending millions of dollars making movies about nothing. What about the movie depicting Black men now scared to leave home without a weapon? What about the movie where there begins a civil war in the United States, between the police and the civilian army put together by the family members of those killed by police when they didn't even have a weapon; regardless of race. What about a movie depicting the entire span of time that an innocent person speeds in jail and is released without a place to take refuge in regular society; (30 years). What about a movie on slavery; everything accurate except the Black people are the owners and the White people are the slaves. Why don't we repeatedly make movies about those who watch and stalk movie stars in the Hills of Hollywood? Why are the famous women mad that hackers took naked pictures of them and posted them on line? I mean they do dance half naked on stage in front of millions and lay in bed naked with other co-workers to become rich. Don't make a movie about a real-life person being molested by their family member and put my face on his or her body?

Just ideas; back to "my life in film":

(I wore clip-on, penny earrings in my nine year old school photo). When I broke the glass in the china cabinet by throwing a brush at my brother, we were both told to remove all of our clothing and wait in our rooms. We were both beat with a switch by our mother. I guess some folks may consider that abuse. This is the only incident like that between me and my brother that I can recall. We never fought each other physically; ever. Not at home or at school; unless we were forced to defend ourselves. Neither one of us has ever been in trouble for starting a fight.

(They say I'm hopeless.....As a penny wit a hole in it....)

Penny played on Good Times and she was physically abused by her birth mother until she was adopted by character, Wilona Woods. If you ask me, I was not abused as a child nor did I feel (ghetto) poor. My city had a reputation for being ghetto because the main mall was situated right next to a conglomerate of apartments. (OK, and because it was just a hop, skip and a jump from city line; the Southeastern part of DC). I lived quite a ways from the mall. Closer to a slightly wealthier city, which is where the youth in our neighborhood attended all 12 years of grade school.

Towson Tigers didn't have the same rep as Georgetown Hoyas. Forestville (Knights) didn't have the same rep as Largo (Lions). Unfortunately, Lionsgate Films and Blue Skye Studios carried the same cross for us to bare as Columbia Pictures and Universal Studios; etc. I don't think this book makes me special. But I invest in me. I took time to write and will take time to ask for your support. If you would give me $1- $5 just because I ask and you know there's a need, why not give me $10-$20 for my book, so that I never have to pan handle ever again?

Look at my volunteer background. I've volunteered with Habitat for Humanity, Christmas in April, and Leukemia and Lymphoma society; at the hospital and library in the region where I grew up; and I've raised money for walk-a-thons with my mother when I was younger. I volunteer to help everyone, with my whole heart. God has a purpose for me. I want to be used by God. Even if it's not inside the church building.

My heart is broken about the fact that I'm literally unable to work now and the reason can't really be proven. My female friends don't want to hang out or invite me to their homes; broken because my daughter never had a dating relationship with her college educated, Christian dad as a little girl and broken because I will never have a best friend or life-mate. But my soul is gutted and completely hollow in knowing that every black person on this planet blames me for my personal business being mangled, rearranged and spread about like a train wreck on television and in movies; even before I made the mistake of believing that men want spontaneity is their sex life. Even before I had sex with a few men I loved and always will remember during my hurtful, forced, homeless situation. (Which should definitely not be an interrogation question years later). If I could change the world..... you would think my love was really something good.....baby if I could...change.....the world.

'We are young. No one can tell us we're wrong. Searching so hard for so long. Heartache to heartache, we stand. No promises, no demands. Love is a battlefield.' I would have to say that we all agree that even in grade school; from their boyfriends; girls want promises and they even try to demand certain treatment. But we accept this entire clause throughout life unless we're lucky.

Lucky. You know the opposite of unlucky; like when you end up working at A.C. Moore, Jerry's Subs and Pizza, or even JC Penney instead of becoming the rich and famous actor you wanted to be.

Chapter 8

My School-Aged Years

I haven't always been homeless. In fact I lived a great childhood and my
early adult life started out plush and very eventful. One might say I felt
very lucky; blessed even.

It was a neighborhood with two entrances. Neither had a sign that let a
driver know that they had arrived. You were now in Ritchie Manor off of
Ritchie Road; where the children went to Ritchie Elementary and in my
home, they lived on Richville Drive and watched the cartoon, Richie
Rich. Our house was small but it had 4 bedrooms and 1 ½ bathrooms.
No dishwasher, no fireplace and no pantry. I can only speak for our
household when I say. We weren't rich, but we didn't want for anything.
Oh, and did I tell you that Woody Wood Pecker lived behind my house?
("No"). Well, he did.

Our neighborhood was full of young kids who enjoyed playing together.
My house was in the back of the neighborhood on the last street. Our
house was in the middle of our street. There was no house directly
across from us so when we hosted our large family for cook-outs, there
was always somewhere to park. The location of our home was great for
kick-ball and dodge ball. The sidewalk was perfect for double- dutch and

roller skating. There was only one thing we had to worry about. The neighborhood terror. This new family moved in two doors down and brought this frightening German Shepard. You would think that they would have purchased a thicker chain or a taller fence. For ten years, he popped his chain and chased the nearest person into a frenzy. He actually bit a few people. You wanna know his name? He has the same name as the toy doll who comes to life and stabs his victims to death. He has the same name as the big mouse with the pizza adventure land for, children's birthdays.

We had a dog for a little while when I was 5. I saw him in pictures. I do not remember kindergarten. I remember far back as second grade because our teacher had a class pet Iguana in our room. He used to pop his chain too but he didn't bite people. Eventually, he ran away. I guess looking back, they were both scared of the animals in the woods behind our homes.

My mother always had birthday parties for me and my brother. It's warm during my birthday and it falls near a holiday and sometimes Spring Break. We would usually not have trouble getting the entire family to come to a cook-out during a holiday; and even our numerous family friends.

My mother used to manage a bank and believe it or not she used to take me to work with her when I was really little; I remember. She was good friends with a lady from India. She shared the name of the puppy on the cartoon Arthur. It was really fun. She eventually left to work for the postal service, like my father. He's worked the night shift ever since I could remember. My mother worked her way up to supervisor but he chose to keep his position and shift. I'm saddened when I think that neither me nor my brother were in a position to take care of our parents the way they took care of us. But at least they had each other after we left.

Although my mom was not a haunted Plymouth vehicle, she drove very fast. That is her name. Christine, like the movie. She called her bosses,

Boss and she was married to a mouse whom she could never catch, in a silent cartoon. Yes that's my dad's name. Well it's just like the ocean...under the moon...; no my brother is not a Spanish singer but he shares his first name. (Give us your heart, make it real or just forget about it).

Our parents worked hard but they played hard too. They loved to travel. When we were young, they took us everywhere. We had a conversion van that allowed us to take road trips in comfort, before gas prices were high and unstable. When we were very young, we flew once and drove down a few years later, to Sea World and Disney World in Orlando, Florida. After my mother's brother was relocated to Wisconsin by his employer, we drove way up there to visit. When I was ten and my brother was sixteen, we drove in a caravan with two other families from the neighborhood, to the World's Fair in New Orleans, Louisiana. Our male cousin who share the name of the son on *The Fresh Prince*, went with us. Everybody had a riding partner. My father or brother rode with me. I forgot to tell you why I couldn't get in the pool at the hotel. A week or so before our trip, I was riding my ten speed with the girl who invited me to play basketball, on the back of my bike. We got up our speed so that when we passed the house with the big dog, we would just sail on by. I didn't work out that way. He was in the front and his bark scared me so much that I crashed my bike. She walked home and I walked my bike home. Bloody and scarred, (obviously discombobulated), I tucked myself into bed. My brother was in his room and my dad was downstairs watching TV. When my mom got home she came in my room and I was bloody and scarred. She yelled at both of them. I couldn't remember where we fell; she asked me. We had to go get my friend and she told my mom what happened. (I didn't have restrictions as to where I could ride within the neighborhood. I wasn't lying. I truly didn't remember). I'm not a doctor so I didn't know that I needed x-rays and a scan of my brain. I had stitches and a big giant bandage on my side. My mom keep it clean and changed my bandage regularly but my trip was not quite as fun as it probably could have been. But it's OK because my brother and I had a lot of stuff around the house to keep us busy. We played cars, Battleship, Connect Four and even had out own arcade sized pinball machine. Every Friday our parents bought dinner from a different carry-out and sometimes we would play Bingo.

Speaking of stiches; my former friend, the surgeon; sister of the anesthesiologist, used to play dolls and house with me and the girls in my neighborhood. Me, her and another little girl, were lying on the ground pretending to be in bed and I needed more space, so I told her to roll-over. She fell down from ground level to the bottom of the basement steps, right in front of the basement door. She busted her chin. We had to rush her to the emergency room. You would think that experience led her to become a doctor but not quite.

Two of my mother's female friend's had a devastating health issue at a much younger age. Fortunately, they survived. The mother of these two previously mentioned doctors, had an aneurism. The mother of the young woman whose first name is my middle name; had breast cancer. They are both still alive and well.

A few years later, for a couple of weeks during the summer, my mom and dad sent me and my brother (alone on a plane) to visit her other brother and his family in Melbourne, Florida. Although he lived in Greece many years before he was stationed in Melbourne, we didn't fly overseas as a family to visit.

I ended up going to Europe in the 9th grade with the French Club. I was taking Spanish, but it was an opportunity that I didn't want to miss. I celebrated my 15th birthday in Europe. It was great. I've never been attacked by a bidet-(*BAPS*). I've never fallen in love with one either-(*Jumping the Broom*). I'd never seen one and I used it once when we first got there. My super fantastic moment of celebration can actually be matched by a super scary moment when I left my purse on the train; in (I believe it was), Switzerland. As I exited the train, I realized my purse was not with me. It had my traveler's checks inside. I don't remember if our chaperone held on to all of our passports or not, but I ran back down the platform and onto the train. I was frantic hoping that the train didn't pull off. I grabbed my purse and rejoined my group. In hind-sight I guess being separated from my group and lost in another country would have been much worse than replacing my traveler's checks.

One day my mother came home from work around 4:30 in the evening and it was pouring down raining. I met her at the door with a towel. I can no longer make it through the day at work. I'm still dancing around the house. I hope she knows that I'm doing the best that I can. My parents never really argued but my brother left. Leaving gave him a second chance. I cry every time I hear the song.

Both sides of my family has always had family reunions on a fairly regular basis. My father's side more frequently than my mom. I don't know which is true. My mother's side of the family stopped having reunions after my mom passed away or after my younger female cousins got married. I think they are all keeping their men locked away for safe keeping.

My father's, mother's, brother's, wife (or his aunt, through marriage) is still living and we are still in touch with that extended family. Meet them. May I introduce them? I only eat the Brown M&M's cause chocolates already Brown. They are very nice and they are all very accomplished. (Mind you; that is the last name of the young lady whose birthday is on September 11th; and my grandmother's maiden name). Our reunion is always the weekend of my grandmother's birthday. I guess I'll see them this fall. (Here's the catch. My only nephew graduates from high school this spring near Tampa. If I ride down there with my dad and stay so that I can move to Miami near my brother I won't make it to my grandson's first family reunion. Who will watch my grandson?)

When I was in elementary school, my father's dad was found dead on the sidewalk out-side of his home. He had apparently fallen or been thrown from his high-rise apartment window. I've never read the police report, however I wouldn't be surprised to find conflicting evidence.

Could the movies, Beverly Hills Cop and I Robot be eluding to the need for a new investigation.

If you are a parent; whether you're obese or not, and you over heard your fifth grader on the phone talking about her boyfriend, would you be devastated. If you had a fifth grader who ate twice as much food during each meal, as your other children; would you be concerned. What if he or she didn't eat vegetables? What about smoking cigarettes or drinking alcohol? Are either of these reasons to stop either child from participating in extracurricular activities? You may not stop them but you definitely need to encourage them. Please keep in mind as you read; I do not have any addictions, nor have I ever. I've never smoked anything or abused alcohol or drugs.

I was invited to go to basketball practice with a friend of mine from the neighborhood when I was 9 years old. (A friend who shares the same last name as the scary family who named their daughter Wednesday). From that day forward I was hooked on the game. (Or maybe I was hooked on all the new friends and fun I was now having). Every season I played a sport with the community Boys and Girls Club. When football time rolled around; I cheered. I played basketball in the winter and softball in the summer. A lot of times, my mother, carpooled a lot of us to practice. We were really good. We had two coaches and one of them was, my (former) best friend and team-mates; father. Our other coach was an older white man who owned a property in Ocean City. Every summer he took three of us to the beach for a weekend. Including our other coach's daughter of course. Life was fun. I only wished I had encouraged my brother to get involved in Boys and Girls Club activities. I wonder why no young men invited him. I wonder what prompted her to invite me.

My mom took us to see Ice Capades every time they came into town.

My mother was like the team mom. She even got an award for being so dedicated to our team; during boys and girls club and high school. My dad worked at night so he missed all of my High school basketball games. The year I ran track; he traveled with us everywhere.

My mom loved to shop. I remember keeping a calendar on my wall logging every outfit; being sure not to wear anything twice in one month during high school. Even when I was smaller I was particular about my outfits. I recall walking through a department store with my mom wearing my all purple outfit to match my newly painted bedroom. (I asked if they could paint my room purple). I was walking with her and she said, "Where is your other shoe?" I said, "It's back there stuck in the escalator." My new purple Jordache sneaker. We went back to get it. I believe I was in the fourth grade.

I remember in elementary school when my mother bought her first dream car. She and my brother picked me up from 6th grade, in a really nice, brand-new, BMW. Unfortunately, my dad totaled it. (Not before my former friend, the Anesthesiologist, used it for her high school prom. But the important thing is that he is OK. His rib broke and punctured his lung. (The actor/actress is driving my mother's car in the movie Machete).

I remember my mother dropping me and my life-long neighbor and friend, (the spice from Gilligan's Island), at bible study on some Sundays. She and I played Barbie dream house in our basements on numerous occasions. We got our first ten-speed bikes on the same Christmas.

The dark side of my basement will always be like the dark side of the moon to me. (.....nothing to do with Mulan). I could never reach my arm around and turn on the light for fear that the monster would get my arm. So I would always fall to sleep on the couch and my brother would come downstairs, pick me up, put me in the bed and tuck me in.

I was taking a lot of dance classes at a small Fashion Institute that was preparing me to compete in the MISS TEEN Pageant; where I won 1st runner up; I was 14. Having the support of an entire community of friends, family and my parents' co-workers, was an awesome feeling. It almost felt surreal, being on stage with that many people clapping for you. (Angelica from the movie; *Six Days, Seven Nights;* my talent: my dance and my out-fit). Well, my hips aren't narrow anymore and my breast may actually be big enough now, too bad I don't look like her. Maybe I could have snagged my green-eyed friend from Wild World Amusement Park.

Oh yeah. That was my first job ever. I met a lot of people. Including my first love. I saw him and wanted to meet him. I was introduced and as I glanced at the other guys in the landscaping department, I immediately became overtaken by another guy. This green-eyed hunk. But it was too late. I composed myself and began a great love affair with the guy who was just as excited to meet me. Guess what happened. My new boyfriend, offered me a ride home. Great! Not great. The gorgeous hunk, was his best friend. He was riding home with us. No I didn't cheat. He was an OK boyfriend. Our mothers talked to one-another and everything. During the summer, he took me to the movies and a few times we returned to work on our day off, to enjoy the fun of the amusement park. Our mother's visited with each other and everything.

He even came to my first dance in high school. I don't remember him inviting me to any of his dances. Our relationship was strained because he didn't attend the same school as I did. Everyone was telling me that he had cheated on me with a girl at his school. They told me her name and everything. I think he must have been just flirting with her. (Oh, a plan to break us up-*High School Musical*). When I wasn't in school I was busy with sports. He was busy in the spring with baseball. They both played for their school. Something in my heart felt different. (Maybe he was mad because he was really overdressed at the Back-To-School Dance). I didn't know he was going to be all dressed up. He never invited me to go out anymore. After a year or so he and I broke up but we were still friends. I had a few other boyfriends during high school. Those relationships didn't last very long. I'm not sure what was said. We talked for a while once and I'm sure we entertained getting back together. But me and my first love ended up 'breaking up for good', (on the phone), right before the prom. I didn't cheat on him or anyone else.

(Might not make sense to you, but it's the world of teen-agers). I decided that we shouldn't go to the prom together. I ended up going alone.

{He led the Redskins to victory in Super Bowl 22. (Just say his name over and over out loud to yourself). I had not long before, had sex for the first time in my life, with my boyfriend-(my first love). But my father sure watches a lot of sports on TV. He could probably draw out some plays. He even looks a little like him}. OMG. So this is the other reason why my high school coach gave me his daughter's jersey number; 22?

For the next year or so, I became closer friends with my ex's best friend. We talked on the phone. It was a while before I actually went over to his home. I think it all started when I found myself talking to him about being mad at my boyfriend years ago when he made me mad.

On prom night, I went to dinner at a restaurant on the water, with a group of friends, (other couples); before the Prom. Guess who I danced with during the first slow song? My Physics teacher. I thought I looked great and I felt beautiful. It was a great night. I went to a Prom after party at a hotel. It wasn't really my scene so I didn't stay long. Then I went to my green-eyed friend's house so he could see how pretty I looked. We slept on the basement floor in front of the TV; fully clothed, all nite; he snuck me in. No we didn't touch. The next morning I went home changed my clothes and went to Kings Dominion with the same group of friends of which I'd gone to the pre-Prom dinner.

Well, he moved to Florida and opened a Fitness Gym. Did I mention that the one and only time he came to my house, when high school was ending; he brought me a roll of cookie dough. He walked in, handed it to me and walked right back out? Yes I knew and still know how to make cookies in the oven, the proper way; I don't need Ingrid from Uptown Girls, to show me. *Clueless*. They're both married; and have been for some time now. Well, anyway....Maybe I'll see him and his family when I go visit my brother. Maybe I won't. Maybe I'll run into my ex when I'm 50, and he'll be single; I doubt it because the last time I ran into him, he was really rude. I'm not sure why. When I ran into him while pan-handling a few years back he came to my hotel and played scrabble with me.

Back to b-ball with my girls:

When it was time for high school, many of us were used to playing ball together so we won a lot of games even though we were short. We made it to the State Championship all four years. We made it; but we came in second every time. (Our coach always said "No one ever remembers who comes in second"). *Welcome Home Roscoe Jenkins*. I don't know what they feed those Broadneck girls; they were all ginormous!

I recall my girlfriend's, sister's boyfriend moving to Colorado. She shares the name of the daughter of the 42nd President. He was in the Air Force and that was where he was stationed. She decided to attend college out there to be near him. Me and my girlfriend flew out to visit her sister during our spring-break. Colorado is absolutely breath-taking. And although her relationship didn't work out and she had a baby before she finished college, she completed medical school on the East-Coast and is now an Anesthesiologist. You go girl!

My mother's friend worked for an entertainment company and was able to get her tickets to some major concerts. During the last two years of high school, during college and a few years after college; me and my mom, were blessed enough to get great seats to the concerts of, Janet Jackson, Michael Jackson and Maxwell. My mother and I went to see Michael but I was able to invite a friend to go with me to see the other artists.

Even though I didn't accept the basketball scholarship to Salisbury, I played intramural basketball at Towson, for fun and exercise. Ok, I should have known to join a media club of some sort even if I wasn't guided to do so. I guess I hadn't really decided what part of Mass Comm I'd desired to work.

I remember speaking with my green-eyed friend who was attending Hampton. He shared with me that he would be transferring to another college because his current school did not have his particular major.

I decided to join a Christian Sorority called ANQ. I recall driving down to Atlanta, Georgia to a Christian Conference with 3 of my frat brothers and 3 of my sorors. There was a snow storm brewing, but we'd already paid our money so we took our time and took turns driving the minivan we'd rented. I was friends with a lot of male and female freshmen on campus. But the new, third-string, freshman quarterback introduced me to my husband. He said we sounded a lot alike when it came to the things of God. No I did not allow him to spend the night. We spent the majority of our time hanging out in my apartment and working out on the track. My soon to be husband, was too busy anyway. He was in and out of town and focused on trying to become a pro-ball player. He was a cornerback. He left school, before graduating to play on the Redskins practice squad. He only had 11 credits to go but that was a chance of a life-time. His jersey number was 22. My jersey number was 22.

During this period, my parents were traveling a lot. Long cruises to the cost of Mexico and other Islands; a trip to Alaska, a trip to Africa. And a train ride across country. Thanks *Home Alone* for the credits that may have led my mom to travel. Who knew she would get sick at such a young age.

Now during my relationship with my soon to be husband, I was very focused on graduating. He was traveling and trying to land a contract with the Redskins. I was wondering why I hadn't been invited to meet his mom and dad yet. Come to find out, his ex-girlfriend had fought with her mom and was staying at his mother's. (He lived there too). His parents didn't know for a long time that there was someone else. He called me from LA one night talking 'bout SHE was with him and she said she was pregnant. I cried for months. He had taken her to the Redskins cook-out while he was supposed to be with me. By the way, you know that girl who sucked the former president's penis; yeah, that was his ex-girlfriends name. (Is that what he wanted from me?) Come to find out, she wasn't pregnant and she left him when he got cut from the Redskins practice squad. He showed up a year later at my door, with flowers; in tears. Against my friends and family member's advice, I took him back. He didn't even have a job. I graduated and found a job as a Reprographics Assistant in the Graphics Department of an Architect firm. I told him that if we were going to continue having sex and he wanted to spend the night, we had to get married. But we planned our wedding. Three months later I was pregnant. I named my daughter after the character in *Mo' Better Blues*. (I was not pregnant when I got married). No, the movie wasn't about me and I've never been to Harlem, but I was dark skinned, and I'd won. It's so sad that things happened the way they did. I, (we), gave up on our marriage so soon. (I wish we'd traveled to an island or taken a cruise for our honeymoon). We went to the Poconos. Can you blame me for trying to form a solid marriage union at an early age?

The new Cinderella movie just came out last week. The light-skinned actor from Mo' Better Blues, shares my last name; in real-life. So I guess she is the real Cinderella. Cause I'm still single. Lol. Maybe I'm still single because an actor/actress whose name in real–life happens to be the same as mine, said in a movie called Waiting to Exhale; when asked about her failed marriage by a fellow actor, that she was not about to go out and find herself a new owner.

Speaking of failed marriage; I suppose the theme song, "Are you that special someone?", from Dr. Doolittle (1998) and the name Blossoms Mammoth Circus; has nothing to do with me being hurt by men who didn't take a relationship with me, seriously (After my divorce). I just noticed the Mammoth Circus scene at the end of the movie, today. May, 2015.

Back on campus:

It seemed as if those who didn't come to school with their best friends, became best friends with their room-mates. My room-mate was from my high-school but, unfortunately she didn't make the grades and lost her scholarship. She was smart but she became a sweetheart to a frat boy and the rest is history. She ended up leaving. She ended up at a larger University and has since graduated and is doing fine. My closest girlfriends had gone to school at Hampton and at MD Eastern Shore where there were a lot of guys from our area and our high school. I wonder if any of my friends ever fell sexually with any of them. I'm kind of surprised that it took them so long to find a life-mate and to have children.

I ended up with a nice White room-mate when I moved off campus. One of my sorors introduced us. She was barely home because she took a job as a nanny for a couple of young children in a neighboring county. I think I sort of pushed her away when I tried to minister to her one day. When she was home, her boyfriend from Bethany Beach was there too. A very attractive black guy. He spent the night quite often. That is not why I ministered to her though.

I remember my parents driving up to my gospel choir concert. It was really nice. My mom also drove up for my induction into the sorority. My pharmacist friend and her mom drove up for the induction as well.

My brother had sort of been coerced into enlisting in the military. He joined the Marines. I know he doesn't regret it. I remember going to his Graduation Ceremony in Parris Island, South Carolina. Soon after, he was stationed in Yuma, Arizona. He told me it was so hot there that you could see the heat rising from the ground. He might as well had been stationed in Africa!.... Well, not quite. You can't take a cross-country road trip home, from Africa. Can you believe he caught the bus home! (One day I hope to drive my daughter cross country to see the west coast). (According to her, she doesn't fly). He'd decided to get out of the military. He married shortly before me but we had our child shortly before them. Long story short, neither marriage worked out.

I was home, he was home, and my entire family came from miles around; crossed states even; to celebrate my daughters first birthday (It was my mother's sister's birthday too). My brother was the clown at her party. That was the theme. It was a cook-out. My daughter's father was there too. Unfortunately my husband didn't take the opportunity that posed itself, to try to rekindle our flame, other than attempting to sleep in the same bed with me. It was clearly over. Can you believe his mother called me talking bout' "he has needs". Not, He loves you and we should try to work it out by going on vacation; but, "he has needs". No, I did not have sex with him.

Now if you think that all of the situations with womanizers in college and the negative outcome with my marriage should make me aware of how volatile relationships with guys can be, you have to wonder why I only am able to have male friends after I return home from a failed marriage. A group of girlfriends rallying around me and helping me thrive again would have been very appropriate. Can't say I didn't try to make that happen.

Apparently, my brother couldn't find a permanent place to live (until he could get back on his feet). Not one family member. I don't remember saying he couldn't live with me and I had literally just gotten keys to my apartment. He and his wife had a son the same age as my daughter and they had recently broken up as well.

I know my brother's heart must have been broken and I feel bad. He doesn't steal and he does not fight. When a black male has one or two negative things happen in the early part of his life; he can definitely begin life with a defeated attitude. Especially if two of those things are as important as shelter, (character) or criminal record, or finance (credit).

He left for Miami. He never moved back to this area. The tears of a clown-when no one's around. I might be cute but I ended up just being a substitute; deep inside I'm blue? Somebody's psychic, Lol.

Deep down in my gut I have a feeling that my brother's sabotage is worse than mine. He told me that he had his own place and a job when he first got there. (He lost his job and never got back on his feet-"he didn't say this to me"-it's just plain to see). He can't work either. (Unfortunately he wasn't keeping in touch with me enough for me to know that his situation had become dire). It's probably because people are harassing him about his sister being a ho. Which I'm not. He has switched rolls with his girlfriend. She works while he stays at home. Sounds like my current life to a 'T'. Well, not to a 'T' cause I'm single. But my daughter thinks she's in the parent roll, because she's working and I'm not. I'm quite sure that no matter where my brother lived; Maryland or Florida; he would not have been able to pan-handle like I'm doing without being beaten by the cops. (When I hadn't heard from him, I went looking for him). I'm a woman and I found myself toe to toe with men who carry guns, (cops); a few times. I guess he and I both are the designated homeless. It's funny because they all think we're jealous of them, (family and friends). Why would everyone be so mean to me and my brother?

I recall flying down to my uncles because we hadn't heard from my brother. I asked my uncle to drive me to Miami. I found my brother in a shelter. He drove back to Melbourne with us. I figured he would be OK from that day forward. By the time I got back home, I understand that he ended up back to Miami. I tried to help. I was living with my parents then. We have all really let my brother down. He was never a menace to society either. (Was I the one who'd found someone who didn't have anything and put em' off on family; family that now live in Newport?) – *Soul Food*. It is a relatively old movie. It would have to be some deep, deep sabotage to try to make scenes from **this movie**; come true. You and I both know, I would never be drinking to get drunk (I don't drink beer) and I would never go after someone else's husband; especially in their home. I don't drink beer. They wanted it to come true so badly, that their husband comes after me. Me and my daughter became homeless because I lost my job. You should never have forced me to move up there.

If I was the person they say. I would be rich from "ho-ing" or stripping. I am not a ho now, nor did I used to be. I just found out what "tricking" meant not too long ago.

OK I know he doesn't consider himself homeless anymore. He found love. I guess homelessness is a little different for military veterans. I hope so.

He loves his family. My brother was never violent in school or in our home. I've visited him several times and even tried to relocate once. I just didn't have the means or the money to do so. I love him. I truly miss him. I hope to live near him one day. He never joined any sports programs or joined any organizations in grade school but he is a very smart, kind person. I failed to mention that I cried all the way home after visiting him in 2004. I did not want to leave him.

Our Christmas' were grand. My mother was a giver. During the earlier part of the year, my brother used to always say something and then say sike. So one Christmas, I got a little box and wrapped it just for him. The only thing it contained was a note stating the word, sike. We all cracked up laughing. (His son sort of reminds you of the guy in the TV show Psyche). And the big brother's T-shirt has nothing but the word sike on the front in the movie- *Diary of a Wimpy Kid*. He and I got along for the most part. We definitely didn't fight like the two boys in this series of movies. Although he didn't used to be the best driver; that is definitely not him in Diary of a Wimpy Kid. He purchased a used old-timer car; you know the thick heavy kind. Unfortunately the brakes gave out and he ran into a police car. (Columbiana). That sounds like a very big ticket to me. If you can't pay your ticket they revoke your license. If you have no license, you have no job. I guess you have to use your personal documents to get a personal identification card. Which may not be as easy as it sounds. But still probably looks bad to an employer. I'm sure this was just the beginning of his problems.

I'm glad that my brother's son had such a fun and rewarding experience in grade school but it breaks my heart to know that my brother wasn't able to be a part of it. Anyone in a position to change his situation, should have. You can't get those precious moments back. Maybe they'll be closer now that his son is older and able to drive himself around.

I'm saddened to think that I can't get the time back that I've lost being so far away from my brother but I can only pray that we will see each other again and be able to enjoy each other's company for however long we have.

Some time ago I began a Small Business Management course at the local community college. I decided not to continue the class but forgot to drop the course. I simply walked away. I unknowingly acquired an 'E' on my transcript instead of what would have been an 'I' for Incomplete.

I took time to go back to graduate school in order to try to reboot myself. I chose a historically Black college to take my graduate level Education courses. Bowie state to be exact. I learned a lot but unfortunately the only class I really enjoyed was the class where the professor was White. But not before driving myself up to Columbia University to speak directly with an advisor about the Master of Journalism program. Although I never became a Broadcast Journalist, *Vantage Point* makes me sort of glad that I didn't. At least not somewhere dealing with political conflict. An actor/actress using my name is being blown-up while reporting. Maybe I can write stories for a newspaper or magazine, from 'home', Lol. I am now writing. I hope to write a few articles and books.

It's 1976 and I am 3 years old. The name of the Steakhouse has changed and our mother's were very close before mine passed away a little over 10 years ago. My middle name is her first name and our profiles are similar. I pray that neither one of our ships are sinking as on April 14, 1912. Although I'm the single parent, that's her mother's name. Her daughter is the one who is hard to impress in the movie Titanic. Is it September 11, 1792? Well, I'm not married. I hope she is.

I'm not feeling very lucky anymore, but I know I'm blessed.

Until We Meet Again

(You can build a castle but you just can't live in it. (My brother the Day Laborer). You're the fastest runner but you're not allowed to win. Doctor says you're cured, but you still feel the pain. (Can't find my mom's cancer because it's behind her stomach). Aspirations in the clouds but your hopes go down the drain. (Me; educated without a job)}.

I feel a world of prosecution against me. I am not the evil, whore-like, (can't take you home to momma), kind of woman that everyone thinks and expresses about me. In the movie, Why Did I Get Married, the guys are bashing some woman named Angela like she is a spawn of Satan.

I know I'm not loud and obnoxious so I wonder what they could possibly mean. I refuse to believe that straight men would actually admit out loud and/or go on television and say that a woman is bad at sex. That couldn't be what they mean. If I were a man in a relationship with a woman whom I knew very well, and she was naked, in my presence and I knew she loved me the way I loved her; I would let her know that I'm a manly man. I would sit down, put her on my lap, slide my penis in her vagina, put her titty in my mouth, grab her butt with both hands, and bounce gently; then I would marry her.

A past boyfriend shared with me that he had gone on a ski trip and met three other men who had slept with me. It was a bus trip. I've been on several ski trips; all as a youngster. I've never had sex on any of them. So to the four guys who didn't even know each other before the ski trip, where they first met; you were obviously all sent there just to meet each other; just to sit in a circle and bash me; (you know who you are). (Four relationships that I'd had over an eight year period several years before I became homeless). You're bad at intimacy and relationships, not me! I'm a woman. I may not have smelled like roses, but I didn't smell bad. I'm not supposed to think to dominate you during intimacy.

Especially if it's our first time having sex. I don't care if you thought you were too small to be on top. Then sit on the side of the bed and take my hand. And if your argument is that I was already lying down, then, that's called foreplay. Roll over and say ride me. It's a confidence that you all just didn't have. You were too worried about having sex with me so that you could call me a ho. And yes, you can have foreplay and not have sex. I believed you loved me; marriage was a given. You win; you happy? The entire world believes I'm a ho. Because I believed you felt the same, I'm unable to work.

You can say that I wasn't confident enough to sit on two people's penises, (in two serious relationships that have already been mentioned, where he was big enough to not need it), instead of sucking them but I can't believe you can't figure out on your own; why that happened. Not because I was pressed for a man or because I needed money or shelter. (I'm homeless and I'm a 'mute'; not mixed, just forbidden to speak, not literally; just figuratively because of the 'one friend at a time rule'). Yes literally! Who do I talk to if he works all day, every day! I am not pressed and I wasn't pressed then. It's never casual to me. I'm not a ho. I sat down on the man I love but my tiny breast weren't facing him. 'Oh yeah'; I'm just bad at sex. In my mind, if you haven't made an attempt to touch my breast in the bed, on the sofa, in the car or stopping me as I walk across the bedroom, why would I think you would touch them in the chair? You were hurting my feelings on purpose. So I'm shunned because I sat down backward? No one's ever taken control in the sitting position. I'm very happy single. For the rest of my life; trust me. Anyway; next topic.

How about the topic of women who go to Florida or New Orleans for Spring Break and sleep with more than one complete stranger while they are there. They return to become professors, consultants, archeologists, accountants, and landscapers. No one cares that they barred their breast and have beads hanging in their bedroom to show for it.

We can talk about *The Ugly Truth* if you'd like. The movie is definitely not about me. Although I did intern with a popular, black owned, radio station and at an advertising agency before I graduated. I remember sharing an elevator with the station owner once; she was nice. I'm assuming her and all of her cohorts love *The Devil Wears Prada* and the new show, being Mary Jane. Unfortunately, there not ugly. I wonder if they like the movie The Best Man.

Besides the one man I'm allowed to be friends with; no one talks to me. For years it's been this way. No one touches me. And neither my daughter nor my father, hug. I guess now for the rest of my life that man will be, my grandson. I guess I'll just talk to him until he's able to talk. I haven't had sex in a little over a year now. Ever since he's been born. (This is not a challenge for me, and never has been). Now I have someone to touch and someone to talk to. I can't stay here any longer without income and I can't take him with me. I pray that my book sells.

But, if I make a purpose to just document all of the things that I do to remind me that I'm alive, that aren't sex; with men, women, children, family members, complete strangers and by myself; It has not been that eventful of a year:

No plans for New Years. No plans for Valentine's Day. I dance around the apartment and outside. I smile a lot. I laugh. I hug people who want to be hugged when it's appropriate. I say good morning and thank you to my bus driver. I quit my part-time job due to verbal harassment from management. Full-time pan-handler again. My first grandchild was born. I became a free babysitter. I kissed my man (of four years); I let him suck on my titty's and stick his finger in my vagina. I broke up with him for good. My family; (my father, my daughter, my grandson and my daughter's boyfriend); took me to dinner for my birthday, to a place I'd already been. My daughter graduated from high school. We took my daughter out to dinner after her graduation. I saw her off to her prom. My daughter was hired as a cashier. My daughter found a job in the government. She's working both jobs. My daughter started college. I No longer have my beat up, used truck. But I still have this completely fabricated parking ticket. Now, how will I ever get my finances straight if the sabotage never stops? I've been given a $500 ticket that has now risen to $600. It was issued in Washington DC. So if I'm unable to get this money by pan-handling, I won't be able to drive. This is an opportunity for my race and Christian folk to come forth and purchase my book in support.

Anyway, what was I saying; oh yeah:

My daughter bought her first used car. We took my daughter to dinner for her birthday. Got my first mammogram. (Having a pronounced lump in my breast, can't be normal). I went to visit my mother's grave. We ordered carry out to eat at the hotel, for my father's birthday when he came into town. My daughter moved into her first apartment. My daughter broke up with her boyfriend, I think. I celebrated Thanksgiving with my extended and immediate family. My grandson had his first Christmas in his home, (my daughter's first apartment). No plans for New Year's. No plans for Valentine's Day. Had a big first birthday party for my grandson, and had a brief conversation on Facebook with my best girlfriend from elementary school; can you believe it; somebody talked to me. She even promised to bring her grandson to my grandson's birthday party. (She didn't show up). I spoke with her the other day and she is getting married really soon. I look forward to celebrating that day with her.

Hooray. My daughter just bought her first brand new car, all by herself. I'm so proud of her. Praise god, she no longer has that used car that can't pass inspection.

After all of this; I would have thought that attorneys would be chasing me. They obviously believe the lies too. When I received the money from my mother's death, they cut my hours. It wasn't that much to begin with. Do you understand what I'm saying? All of the children were literally acting like baboons so that none of the teachers would request me as their substitute. The S.I.M.S system couldn't help if the teacher didn't want you as their substitute. When you work all day, it's hard to find time to write a book or file a lawsuit without an attorney that you can't afford. It's also hard to find time and energy to go to the movies. When you work hard all day, you get home and you just want to stay there. Even when you're homeless; after a full day of pan-handling, you're tired. Entertaining company is great but going out and partying at night is not likely. (Can't have female company if no females ever talk to you.) The libel and slander that causes defamation, has always bothered me. And has always been successful at keeping me from maintaining friends and prospering.

Heavenly father; I refused the white man's invitation to move to a bordering county, only to be used by a few ignorant black people when I needed shelter after losing my job in the school-system; (No it was not casual to me). This book wasn't written to give excuses for why I had sex while I was homeless. No, I wasn't just doing what I had to, to survive. I think a part of me just wanted to see if someone could really be that evil. Wow; after all black people had been through. It truly makes me not want to vote for anyone Black, ever again. I am not a ho. I don't have sex so I can enjoy the feeling of cumming. And I do not sleep with people for employment, money or shelter.

As a classroom of my students chanted one day; during a conversation about "my" sex-life; that they held amongst themselves as if it was part of the curriculum; "Nobody had a gun to her head." Assuming that everything they've seen is about me. But I know, I wasn't ho-ing. Because I don't even know what ho-ing is. Seven years. One teacher boyfriend whom I dated and became intimate with; in the entire school system. He invited me to fly with him to Europe, but I don't fly any longer; I'm claustrophobic. (I know I need to stop confessing that.) I guess your attempt to get me out of the country didn't work.

Here is where I attempt to begin a writing career. I'm quite sure you're having a focus group on how to sabotage this. It's almost flattering.

Trying to replace public shame with 'something else', is not the same as telling the truth after you've been lied on for 20 to 30 years to protect someone else's feelings. When your spouse watches *Bridesmaids* and sees me riding the male actor instead of you, in the back of his mind; that's a problem. That's not normal.

I mean think about it. I traveled to and returned from Europe, a virgin at age 15. The only movie that I know of, that really focuses on a young female virgin that age 15, is the one where a 15 year old virgin goes to Europe, gets kidnapped and is used as a sex slave. *Taken.* Maybe I was cast and stuck in the movie Django.

Let me just say this. When I was in elementary school, there was a girl who smelled really bad, every day. No one wanted to sit next to her. I'm quite sure she didn't have a boyfriend. Even though I'm sure the teacher already knew, we finally told the teacher so that the teacher could let her know. We didn't tease her. We weren't mean to her.

The way I smell is not provable. Because people lie. Now supposedly, in a small house, in an area where there are three tables with at least 25-30 dishes of food; on Thanksgiving, I smell bad. I entered the house not smelling. The point is supposed to be that I need to change my pad more frequently. Now afterward, I rode with my father in his pickup truck. I didn't smell anything. But supposedly, he did. I know if I smell fishy and I know if I smell like urine. I'm not saying this because it hurts for people to tell me I smell. They are all being ridiculous. I'm not crying because the truth hurts. I'm crying because everyone believes the lies and others continue to tell more lies.

Please remember; Conditioning is science. Science is exact and provable. However, it becomes a weird science when you use it in the wrong way.

My hair is healthy because I care for it. My teeth are healthy because I care for them. My skin is clear because I care for it; also because I have regular bowel movements. I'm at peace when I'm alone because my spirit is full of real love, always. After an unprofessional person infected my toenail, I tended to it regularly and it's getting better. Why would I not pay attention to the way my underarms or vagina smell?

If I've always worn a pad that I don't change regularly enough and I consequently smell, how was I able to meet all of these men to even talk and hang out and sometimes kiss, for the past 30 years? The women are now attempting to answer this question as I walk around and pan handle. Either they're not very smart or it makes them feel better about themselves to believe and say to me that they "don't have any change right now but they may or they will when they come out", (of the grocery store). Implying that I'm single because I smell after sex. There's a lot of other reasons to not be able to get or keep a man, when you're unemployed and homeless. But if the entire population believes your hygiene is bad, you will probably be unemployed and homeless forever. That's their goal remember, to keep me in loser status.

All of the movies are not an exact truth about me. (I'm not you and you're not me). Pay attention to each movie you watch and understand the message that is meant for you. And if it's not exactly true, it's exactly false.....Yeah, there's Hertz and there's not exactly. Just because it hurts; that doesn't mean it's true. That has nothing to do with the things that your children see on TV and use as fuel to harass his or her teacher, as you sit by and condone it. I've made mistakes. Let it go.

(You may think I'm crazy, and you are entitled to your opinion. Just please don't harass me with your opinion.)

Now say, "All this, and now she's writing this because she's hurt"? As if going on a shooting rampage would have been the better choice when I first saw the group of movies attempting to sabotage me. So which response do you want? Now try to sue me for my money if I earn any from the book that exposes the breach of my civil rights. What response do you think you'll get from that? Prayerfully; divine intervention. Not the reaction the actor/actress gave in "Why Did I Get Married."

My heart is broken because my cousins and former girlfriends don't want to go out or invite me to their homes. My heart is broken because my daughter never had a dating relationship with her college educated, Christian father. My heart is broken at the thought that I will never have a best friend or life-mate. My heart is broken because I should never be interrogated by anyone about why I had sex with a few men whom I loved in different ways than typical, and will never forget, during this hurtful, **forced** homeless situation that has not yet ended. But my soul is completely gutted and left hollow at the thought that every black person on this planet exhales with satisfaction in knowing that my life's story has been mangled and thrown about like a train wreck; even before I made the mistake of believing that men wanted sexual spontaneity in a relationship.

What I thought was a great way to get to know someone before you become intimate, was completely ignored during the process of harassing me. A typical date is dinner and a movie, I guess. When I was invited to live with my ex-boyfriends sister after being left outside; we all drove home together and then played board games until mid-nite; for about a month. I made it clear then, that I didn't want to play house and that I wasn't a ho. You can learn a lot about someone by playing Taboo or Scattergories. He would visit me during his lunch–time if I wasn't already busy pan-handling. There were a lot of other reasons why the relationship ended and I do not believe I was at fault. I am not a cheater. I did not cheat on him. I was put in the role of a homeless woman who was lied to by her boyfriend. That doesn't make me a ho. The majority of the time I live in the hotel I paid for. And the men I stayed with did not come on to me or pretend to make me a girlfriend. Yeah a few men lead me on but I wasn't ho-ing. Don't get it twisted.

The men from past relationships, prior to me being homeless, can lie and say that the reason why our relationship didn't work out is because I smelled but that is an enormous lie. I remember the first time I smelled after intimacy. It was after I became homeless. Very rare. Only a few times and it was because I'd had a miscarriage from a previous pregnancy in a previous relationship. I didn't look pregnant. I was pudgy but wearing two winter coats to stay worn can create a really fat torso. (I had gotten pregnant by my 7 year on and off relationship partner). And no I don't need to refresh more, I need to enjoy my life more.

Is there one decent person who is able to assist me in my attempt to earn a living and keep a roof over my head, without a male life-mate and without sleeping on my daughter's sofa? Working a nine to five, is not an option. Writing for a newspaper or magazine from home is an option. Doing hair in the basement of my home is also an option.

I have a lump in my breast and I have no health insurance. I'm paying monthly to my Insurance carrier just to get a yearly check-up. I'm supposed to pay for everything else. I have no money. It's murder. I do not now, nor have I ever intentionally cheated with the intent of deceiving my mate. I have never intentionally tried to break-up someone else's marriage. I would never intentionally share a man. I would never intentionally be a ho. Please help me. I don't need you to predict what I'm going to say or do and then say I'm repeating you. I need you to help me get through the sabotage of having no income, etc. I am not obeying commands, although I have been conditioned to a certain extent. I remember my mother saying, "If I listen to the doctors, I'd just be sitting around crying all day." I guess that's why she continued working and tried to stick to her usual routine. Well, I just watched the movie called A Joyful Noise and if I sit and watch movies and listen to secular or gospel music all day, I'd probably sit around crying all day too. The information that is being twisted and misleading to viewers. Oh my God. It's overwhelming.

You called yourselves getting me back when I didn't know enough math to teach. You stuck my daughter in classrooms with long-term substitutes who didn't lecture or give out homework. You did that to my daughter because you thought I was a prostitute. I went to graduate school for a refresher course and to prepare myself for the classroom.

This is a shout out to all department heads in every school on every level. Meet with your long–term substitutes to go over what is being taught and the progress of the academic goals on a weekly basis. Don't make them have to try to hunt you down.

To all the single ladies, whether you've been married or not; knowing that it is your desire to be married, I would never say to you, you are single because you smell or because you are just a ho. I can confidently say that; knowing that anyone who is reading this, 270 page book, is not retarded.

For those of you who are a little slow or love challenged; let me break it down for you. I'm not more in love with any man right now, over another; I do not have a man. Each asshole had a chance to convince me that he was worthy of my love. I believe that God wanted me to be with the man who took vows with me or the man with whom I lost my virginity, if I choose to be with a man at all. My heart was always been open for love and marriage but I'm happy single. Lord forgive me for cursing. I want to be used by God. I truly want to enjoy the company of a friend. Male or female.

I've never had sex with two people at once but even if I decided to have sex with three people at once, it's none of your business. I may not be an angel in your eyes but I'm not an un-repented sinner.

There's the voice of men saying it's too late to say all of this, you should just wait longer in your relationships with men. That didn't work either. I did not necessarily need to list the men I did not sleep with to try to prove that I'm not a ho.

Let me guess. After publishing the truth in this book, I won't be hired by those who violated my rights in the first place? (Don't be ridiculous. You never had a chance to be hired by such large companies in the first place.) Even though they made movies like Juwanna Mann that have the main character in my jersey number, on a female basketball team. I'm not an exhibitionist. I'm not conceited or rude. And I've never made out with any basketball team-mates. **The office scene they show, up against the desk; that is identical to that in the movie Hitch; is not true.** Juwanna's hair, as a man, is strikingly similar to how mine was cut and styled after my divorce. His female co-stars hair is like mine in my actual basketball picture. Her movie boyfriend is the real-life cousin of my ex from high school whom I met up with after my divorce. He was the one who'd just purchased the new Cadillac. I've just seen the movie for the first time, May 2015.

Yes Disney, for some reason, I've lost all of my friends. Earlier when I spoke of being shunned, I still hadn't seen the movie yet. Attorneys chase ambulances. Why didn't they come find me? Oh, they sent a Black female attorney to come and get a bikini wax from me. That's not why I'm single. Clearly, everybody wants me to stay broke.

In *Diary of a Mad Black Woman*. That's my rich doctor; former friend's hand-me-down car from her dad. And 'my' favorite spot (restaurant) in the world; that's her name. (I'm not saying this to be disrespectful).

Yeah Disney, it's "Girl Meets World". I guess it's hard to take on the world when the entire world is misled!

Our (20 year) neighbors to the right share the last name of the capital of Texas. The youngest son married a stripper. He was warned to be careful by the 'Knight' in *Pretty Woman*. He's the spitting image of the dark-skinned guy with the locks from *The Best Man*. Before their father died last year, he told me I was invited to live with all of them in N.C.. He still lived here and he knew I was homeless. Had I moved in with them, she would have known that she was his dream, because I would have been there.

Ok so I'm sleeping on my daughter's sofa. I know the saying, beggars can't be choosy. But can I have my life back please? I'm getting messages from those around me, I suppose from those who've violated my rights, that it's too late to sue them or tell the truth. So I suppose if no one purchases my book, I will just be homeless forever.

I've been given an ultimatum by planet Earth. Either I can befriend drug-dealing, whore-minded, uneducated folks or I can sit and stare at the wall for eternity. I think I'd better go get my mother's beautiful artwork and hang it up. Not because they think I sold sex but because they believe I had sex too easily with too many people.

Had I married the thick, dark-skinned Black guy in Brown Sugar, who was singing "The ho is mine", my name would have been: The Keys In 'A. Minor'. Are you familiar with the album? She's never met me or even held a conversation with me; but this album made her a millionaire.

No 'Love Doesn't Cost a thing' and yes I had my first car accident in front of **Morgan** State University while in college. My father told me that my car sustained **$3,000** worth of damage. He was the one who changed my brakes, my oil, and showed me how to change a flat tire after I'd gotten stranded and couldn't change it myself. My mother passed away a few months before this movie was released. I suppose they care about my father and did not want him to have unprotected sex. Or were they mocking the fact that I bought a box of condoms before I visited California for the first time. Did not have sex when I got there; but I had condoms. I never buy condoms. (And no I was not expecting to have sex). I'm sure I could have found someone if that were my desire. Bottom line; I didn't pay anyone and no one paid me, for sex; ever.

I can't walk past stationary Jehovah's witnesses at the subway station without hearing; "Oh now you're a ho". (...from the woman) and, "Well what was it then?"(...from the man). (It is May 2015) Everyone thinks I smell. Excuse me; smelled in every relationship I've had. They believe that the plane crashes and train derailments are because I know people and I'm hurt because no one wants me. I can't sit on the metro bus without the person behind me saying out loud; "Cause you're a ho."

My first book is a poetry book and I would like to deliver copies that I've finally had completed, to churches; and I would like to go to certain people's homes to ask for a purchase of support. My daughter told me to take her car yesterday to pan-handle all day but she will not allow me to drop her at work and keep her car tomorrow so that I can sell my poetry book. Is it me or does it seem like I'm being held against my will to keep me poor? It is now a consensus among all humans that I am unfit to be in a healthy, monogamous relationship. No man is interested. It is May 2015. I am to come to grips with 'never having hope' for finding my very own man.

I just saw the movie *Hope Floats* for the first time (May 2015). This movie came out in 1998, when I was newly divorced and sometimes hosting male company in my apartment. I'm being indirectly told as I watch this movie that everyone knew then, that the actor/actress was portraying me. See I had a little girl and I was single. They believe that I needed to wash up before intimacy, as portrayed by the actor/actress. Then many years later I'm allegedly sitting on the counter in my apartment, alone, asking why no one wants me; as shown in *Miss Congeniality* by the same actor/actress. It doesn't bother be that they are obsessed with me in Hollywood but I wish I knew that everyone believed all of these things about me before I attempted to develop a relationship with those men whom I welcomed into my life. (This is where the ignorant, childish, random comments of, "Well what was it then?", come from. No, I've never had sex in a white oxford shirt with no bottoms; *Hope floats* and *Notorios BIG*.

Could the showing of the movie *Hope Floats* last night and the fact that I can't tread water, but just flip and float on my back, be a sign that the young woman I met yesterday while pan-handling, who has her own indoor playground not far from here, will really be able to HELP me get my writing career going by assisting me in promoting my poetry book. I consider this Devine intervention and beneficial networking.

When you see me cry, know that my tears are not falling for the reason you probably think. But I see that it gives you great joy to think I'm not happy and that you can cause great misery in my life; say what you will to make yourself look and feel better. If I were a ho I would say so. I have no one to answer to but God.

Read this book again. Pay attention. Believe and understand what you've read here, as you've believed that trash you've read previously by other authors. Then change your ways. I'm not a ho. It's you who needs to change. My conscience is clear and it always has been. Is yours?

Do you all really believe that finding the perfect man for me and/or, me not having to work, can heal the pains of an entire world stabbing me in my back? Although I have yet to receive that large wad of money, one may say, I'm no longer clueless. All of the clues that I've been given, have made me more aware. The significance of the letters **BP** and the movie **300**. Stop *Changing Lanes* so you won't *Crash*. The **black and white** bunny cartoon characters with the big breast and the woman with the big nose, who shares my middle name as her first; being the **base pair** because both have fathers whom were in the military. The other woman will have big breast and I have an ugly nose; so I will not win in a competition for a man. Am I warm yet or am I getting colder? From what I've read, it appears that this **horrible disease; (HIV)** can live in ones system for a long time. I praise God that I don't have it. And I purpose in my heart to find a way to remember every day, those who died from it and those who are still living with it. I Love You and May God Continue to Bless You.

ABOUT THE AUTHOR

I was born in Washington DC. I grew up from age 2 in a suburban neighborhood called Forestville; in Prince George's County Maryland. I graduated from Largo High School and Acquired a Bachelor's Degree in Mass Communications from Towson State University. I worked to pay my way through Cosmetology school soon after I graduated from college. I was very athletic and I still exercise and try my best to eat right. I married right out of college and got pregnant right away, with my only child. I took graduate courses for a year to change careers and then lost my job. (I was set up). Unfortunately, my marriage ended. In my lifetime, I have traveled over-seas and to the west coast of the United States. I've been as far south as Florida and Louisiana; as far north as Wisconsin and New York. I am a single, live in nanny for my only grandchild. If this situation does not work out, I will be homeless. I am enjoying the beginning of my writing career; my first passion. Writing is my only form of income. I am a pan-handler in the region where I grew up. I am not a felon nor am I disabled; but I am unable to work. The reason why I believe historians need to read and document this work is because this is an unprecedented amount of humans who call themselves followers of the all mighty God, who have intentionally left me separated from my only child; to rot. An overwhelming amount of people who believe they are smart, who are blithering idiots. And a big group of folks who say they are nice but are really mean as hell. Remember; I was told by a male stranger who took me in, that if I would not sleep with him that I had to leave. This was said after I'd already stayed there for an entire week. I left. It wasn't until I slept with a man whom I'd met while homeless; did evidently, the cult who orchestrated this non-sense; find a permanent home for me and my daughter. They also offered her a job. The only time I was physically assaulted was when I lived in the home of a strange woman who turned out to be an alcoholic. Why the f—k would I want to live with a strange man! May God have mercy upon your souls.

ANGELA C. WILLIAMS